Spelling
Smart Junior

The Princeton Review

Spelling
Smart Junior

by Gary Arms

Random House, Inc.
New York

Princeton Review Publishing, L.L.C.
2315 Broadway
New York, NY 10024
E-mail: comments@review.com

ISBN 0-679-77538-2

Editor: Gretchen Feder
Production Editor: Kristen Azzara
Designer: Evelin Sanchez-O'Hara
Production Coordinator: Evelin Sanchez-O'Hara

9   8   7   6   5   4   3   2   1

Acknowledgments

The author would like to thank Evan Schnittman for asking him to write this book. He would also like to thank his editor, the smart and hard-working Gretchen Feder. He'd also like to thank all The Princeton Review staff who worked on this book, including Kristen Azzara and Evelin Sanchez-O'Hara, and Neil McMahon.

Contents

Introduction for Parents

Spelling Smart Junior grew out of a couple of important realizations:

1. Many commonly used English words are very difficult to spell. Even good spellers often misspell these words.

2. Most books that are designed to help students become better spellers are never read. Why not? Because they are boring!

We at The Princeton Review decided that *Spelling Smart Junior* would be different. We created a book that is fun to read.

Spelling Smart Junior tells a fun story, which is designed to make it easy for students to become good spellers. Kids will be entertained by this funny and exciting adventure story and naturally learn the spelling techniques and tips that are embedded within it.

Spelling Smart Junior focuses on the words that kids and ordinary people actually use in their writing. It's easy to generate lists of obscure words that nobody uses, but what good are they? This book focuses on the words kids really use and are most likely to misspell. It teaches students how to stop repeating their mistakes in the writing they do for school.

The early chapters tell the truth about spelling English words. Spelling is difficult! Some words are so tricky that even English teachers and professional writers often make mistakes when they use them. These chapters focus on explaining why so many commonly used English words are hard to spell, and they teach students specific techniques that are proven to be effective ways to learn new words. The middle chapters focus on the fifty-five words most commonly misspelled by junior high students. The last third of the book focuses on more than one hundred words that nearly everyone (including smart parents) commonly misspell. Each chapter ends with helpful exercises and quizzes. (The answers are in the back of the book.)

Finally, what is the best way to help your child improve as a speller? Get involved. Care. Encourage and praise. In any kind of learning, nothing matters more than motivation. A parent can do a tremendous amount for a child just by caring, paying attention, and offering encouragement. How can you help? Work with your kids to figure out the words they frequently misspell. After they complete the exercises at the end of each chapter, check their work with them. Help them with the spelling quizzes in this book. If your student has any level of success, praise her and tell her she's learning a lot. If a student learns how to spell one new word correctly, that is an accomplishment and deserves praise! And if it turns out that your own spelling improves as you help your child, well, that would be great too!

Introduction
for Kids

Hey kids, this is a serious warning!

Don't read any further, unless you want to meet the following:

- a good-looking, fun-loving kid named Biff, who is in danger of being executed at dawn, unless he can learn to spell the fifty-five words junior high students most commonly misspell

- a giant dog named Woof, who is said to be trained to capture bad spellers and drag them to a dungeon

- a finicky Duchess of Rules, so crazy about rules that she wants to reform the entire English language

- a Guard of Spelling, who carries a sword and may possibly be totally insane due to mysterious reasons

We mean it! Be careful!

Don't read any further, or you will be in serious danger of meeting the following:

- a tall, sarcastic girl named Beth, who does not seem entirely honest

- a mysterious King and Queen, who live in a maze-like palace full of strange rooms

- a crazy guy in a chicken suit, who turns out to be one of the richest men in the world

Close this book now, close it quick or you will discover the following:

- a dungeon containing a trapdoor
- a mysterious tower
- a brilliant green parrot missing some tail feathers
- a monkey, who will do just about anything to learn to fly

But most of all, shut this book right away or you could actually *learn* to do something:

- YOU COULD LEARN TO SPELL!

In this book, the Smart Junior kids, Barnaby, Babette, and Bridget, find out that Beauregard, the talking cat, has a serious spelling problem. To help him learn to spell, they take him to a mysterious Palace of Words but once there, everything begins to go wrong. Before they know it, they are up to their necks in an adventure full of danger and excitement, love and laughs.

Maybe everything turns out happily; maybe it doesn't. All we can say for sure is that if you read this book, you will learn to spell lots of words, and you definitely won't get bored!

Chapter 1:
Beauregard's Dark Secret

Was English spelling designed to make people go crazy?

Beauregard wished he had something to do. Barnaby was here; Bridget was here. But all they were doing was sprawling around Bridget's living room eating potato chips and watching something dumb on TV. Pretty soon Babette would arrive. Maybe something would happen then. Usually when these kids got together, it did not take long before they were all involved in some serious antics. Beauregard smiled his cat-grin and wiggled his long whiskers. If the kids did get into trouble, it would be his duty to save them. He imagined a giant, ferocious dog snarling at his friends. Then he imagined rising up on his hind legs and hissing at the giant dog, and the dog yelping and running for his life.

Now, that would be an exciting adventure. Beauregard imagined the kids thanking him for saving them from the dangerous canine. He wiggled his long whiskers. Beauregard was a cat, a very large black one, but he was no ordinary cat. For one thing, he could talk.

"Is that the door?" he asked, addressing his question to no one in particular.

Barnaby grunted. Bridget said, "I didn't hear anything." Barnaby ate a potato chip. Bridget unwrapped a piece of bubble gum and stuck it into her mouth. She was very fond of bubble gum.

Beauregard thought, if none of these kids gets into trouble, and quick, I am going to fall asleep from sheer boredom.

The doorbell rang. Beauregard leapt out of his chair and ran over to it. He did not care who it was, he would be glad to see anyone.

Bridget also jumped up. "I'm coming!" She straightened her baseball cap so that its brim faced backward, just the way she liked it.

The doorbell rang again, loud and hard as if the person on the other side of the door was in a big hurry.

"I said I was coming, didn't I?" Bridget said. Before the doorbell could ring a third time, she yanked open the door.

Standing in the doorway was a slender, attractive girl dressed all in black. She wore very cool sunglasses that were so black, no one could see her eyes.

"Babette!" yelled Bridget. Babette was one of her very favorite people in the whole world.

"I'm mad," said Babette, her French accent more pronounced because of the anger she spewed. She strode into the room. "I am furious, angry, perturbed, and upset."

Barnaby jumped up. "Why? What's the matter? Are you okay?"

"Look at this insult!" Babette pulled a piece of paper out of her purse and waved it in the air.

"What is it?" Barnaby asked. His thick, bushy hair stuck up every which way.

"A poem," Bridget said. "A perfectly beautiful poem that I submitted to one of your famous poetry magazines."

"I didn't know you even wrote poems," Bridget said. "Cool." She admired her friend tremendously; there was no end to all the cool things that Babette did. She could speak several languages fluently, for example, and had traveled all over the world.

"I guess they rejected it, huh?" Barnaby said. He was not all that crazy about poems, but he hoped Babette didn't get her feelings hurt.

"I don't mind the rejection," Babette said. "I can take a little rejection."

"Everybody gets the door slammed in their face from time to time," said Bridget. She thought of offering her friend a stick of bubble gum, then thought better of it. The French girl was a little too cool to appreciate the wonderfulness of American bubble gum.

"It is the insult that makes me mad!" yelled Babette. "Look at this!"

On the piece of paper were several large, red marks. Someone had circled several of the words in the poem with a red marker.

"They circled my mistakes! How rude; how perfectly unforgivable! Oh, I hate your language, your stupid English. It is impossible to spell!"

"Wow," said Bridget, "they really nailed you, huh?" She looked carefully at the piece of paper. Although Babette's poem was neatly typed on good paper, it did contain several spelling errors. Because Bridget was an expert speller, she recognized the mistakes the moment she saw them. "You should've let me proofread this Babette."

Beauregard sniffed haughtily, "Oh well, spelling." He sniffed again to show his utter contempt. "It doesn't matter, not in the least. Spelling is stupid."

The three kids whirled around to look at the cat. He seemed a little startled to get so much attention.

"Well, it is stupid," he repeated firmly. "No one with any sense cares at all about spelling!"

"English spelling is designed to make people go crazy," Babette agreed. "If you ask me, your so-called spelling system was invented by a mad scientist."

Because Barnaby was a science whiz, he did not exactly like this statement. "Now, wait a second..." he sputtered.

"I would not be surprised if some dogs are at the bottom of this," suggested Beauregard, interrupting Barnaby. He waved his tail ferociously to indicate his contempt for the mad scientist dogs that had probably invented English spelling just to drive human beings crazy.

"It is sort of weird," Bridget laughed. In a way, this was a funny kind of topic to be discussing, but she did want to calm down Babette. "Did you ever see this word?" On a piece of paper, Bridget wrote in big letters: GHOTI. She held up the piece of paper so the rest of them could all see it. "What's it spell, huh?"

"It doesn't spell anything," said Barnaby.

"Who cares what it spells?" demanded Beauregard. He thought, maybe it spells something that has to do with a goat.

"We all give up," Babette said. "What does it spell?"

"Fish!" Bridget said triumphantly. "G–H–O–T–I spells fish!" She laughed loudly.

"Fish?" Beauregard was an awful speller, but he could hardly believe that this crazy combination of letters could possibly spell the word "fish."

"G–H as in 'tough' or 'rough,'" Bridget explained. "O as in 'women.' And T–I as in 'motion.' G–H is the 'f' sound. O is the 'i' sound, and T–I is the 'sh' sound! That adds up to FISH!"

"That adds up to total insanity," said Beauregard. "As I said before, spelling is stupid."

Once again, the others turned around and gave him a long, hard look.

"Barnaby," asked Bridget, "are you thinking what I'm thinking?"

"I can't believe it," Barnaby said.

Even Babette seemed surprised. "Why, Beauregard, my sweet, can it be true?"

Beauregard looked uncomfortable; he squirmed, waved his tail, and nervously looked out a window. "I think I see an interesting bird out there," he said, trying to distract them.

"Beauregard!" yelled Bridget. "You're a lousy speller!"

"It is nothing to be ashamed of," said Babette. "It is not your fault that English spelling was invented by a crazy person."

"It's probably because you never write anything," Bridget said. She didn't want to make her friend Beauregard feel bad. "It's hard to hold a pencil or use a keyboard with those big paws."

"Creative spelling," Beauregard said airily, "is characteristic of a gentleman—or in my case, a gentle-cat."

"It is not!" Bridget said. "It's a problem, one you should work on. Anyone can be a good speller if he just works on it."

Barnaby had pulled a book off a shelf and was rapidly turning the pages.

"What's he got?" asked Babette. "The telephone book?"

Beauregard sighed. Now, he was in for it. His dark secret was out. He knew these kids. Bridget, Barnaby, and Babette would not rest until they turned him into a good speller. Who knew where they would wind up? Well, at least it would get them out of Bridget's apartment. After all, he had been longing for an adventure. Maybe it wouldn't be so bad.

"Find anything, Barnaby?" he asked.

Barnaby opened the telephone book to Spelling. There was only one entry. He read it out loud.

"The Palace of Words. Spelling Is Our Specialty (also Reading and Writing). Everyone Welcome! Especially YOU!"

Barnaby rubbed his bushy, bristly hair. "Anyone want to investigate?"

Ten minutes later, they were on a bus.

"I figure it's some kind of store maybe," said Barnaby.

"Or a clinic," teased Bridget. "A brain surgery clinic. I guess old Beauregard here will need a transplant—a brain transplant!"

"Now Bridget," said Babette, "there's no need to tease. When it comes to spelling your insane language, everyone needs a little help." In fact, Babette figured she could use quite a bit of spelling help herself. She thought of the red circles on her poem and blushed.

"My other guess is that it is some kind of private school," Barnaby said, "a place where you can obtain the services of an excellent tutor."

The cat looked gloomily out a window. He knew that he was one of the world's worst spellers. He spelled by ear, sounding out the words, and the result was often...well...downright embarrassing.

"If we get a tutor," Babette said, "I wonder if he will be cute. What do you think, Bridget? I find I learn best from the cute tutors, don't you?"

Bridget blushed. In fact, her favorite teacher was a plump man with a large bald spot. Even his own mother would never dream of calling Mr. Gonzalez "cute." He was funny though, and his bright eyes never missed a thing.

"End of the line!" yelled the bus driver. "This is where you kids get off. And take that cat with you!"

The kids and Beauregard jumped out of the bus. With a big puff of diesel smoke, the bus disappeared.

"It's kind of dark," Bridget looked around at the strange street. "Kind of foggy."

"Are you sure this is the right place? That bus driver got out of here so fast, you'd think he was scared or something." Barnaby rubbed his hair.

"Hey, what's that?!" yelped Beauregard.

Two dark figures were approaching.

Exercise for Chapter 1:
Make a List of YOUR Spelling Errors

Most kids—most people really—make the same spelling mistakes over and over. The mistakes you make in your everyday writing are the ones that really matter. After all, if you never use a word in your writing, you are not going to have the opportunity to misspell it. The words that get you in trouble are those you use all the time but spell incorrectly. Even good spellers make some mistakes. As far as they are concerned, those mistakes *look* fine. They don't even catch the mistakes when they proofread.

One of the best ways to become a good speller is to make a list of the words you tend to misspell. To do this, you need help. You need a good way to find your errors so that you can make them into a list.

Maybe someone else who is a great speller can help you find the words you misspell. Is your mom or dad good at spelling? Do you have a friend who is a great speller? What about your English teachers? Teachers are trained to find mistakes. They do it all the time. Does your English teacher draw circles around your mistakes? Don't throw away those assignments. If your teacher circles the words you spell incorrectly, you should do something really crazy and thank her. She will probably faint. But after she wakes up, she will realize you are just trying to improve your spelling.

If you use a computer to do your writing, always use the word processing program's spell-checker. Spellcheckers are not too smart. They can't really read, and they definitely will not catch all your mistakes. But most kids find that spellcheckers do catch a lot of errors. Although they aren't perfect, they can definitely help you find many of the words you misspell consistently.

Compile a list of spelling mistakes you make in your regular writing and work on them. If you can learn to spell the words on your list correctly, you will soon eliminate tons of your mistakes!

Chapter 2:
The Palace of Words

How many words in the English language can you list that are spelled without the letters A, E, I, O, or U?

The two dark figures emerged from the fog. It was a little old man and a very tall old woman. The two old people looked so kindly and friendly that Bridget thought she wouldn't mind having them for grandparents.

"Come on, Mom," said the chubby old man. "We'll be late. In fact, we are already late! Oh dear, oh dear."

Seeing the kids and Beauregard, the old woman stopped. "Pop, hold up a moment."

The old man stopped in his tracks so abruptly that a notebook fell out of his pocket. He was wearing a vest covered with pockets, and every pocket contained pens, pencils, or pieces of chalk. Other pockets contained small writing notebooks, and some held tiny paperback books.

"Hello there!" Mom smiled cheerfully at Babette. "You kids aren't lost, I hope."

"You know what?" Barnaby picked up the dropped notebook and returned it to the old man. "We are lost!"

Beauregard took a step forward. "We are only a little lost. Perhaps you can help us, sir. Or you, ma'am."

"My goodness." Pop stared at Beauregard so hard his eyes nearly popped out of his head. "Darling, I thought that animal, that really rather handsome cat—you'll think I've gone silly, but I thought he…"

"Spoke!" cried the old woman. "He spoke!" I heard him clear as a bell!"

"I am Beauregard," the cat said. "At your service, sir, ma'am." He bowed grandly.

"A talking cat," said Pop. "Isn't that wonderful, Mom? Isn't that perfectly amazing?"

"No matter how wonderful and amazing it is," said Mom, "we can't stop. We promised the school children. We can't delay, not another minute." She reached down and tapped the old man's shoulder.

"What a pity, dear. It is most unusual to encounter a talking cat. But an appointment is an appointment, and a promise is a promise."

The old couple suddenly turned and began to scurry down the sidewalk, then stopped. Both of them spun around. "Oh, fudge," said Pop. "We forgot to say good-bye."

"Oh, fudge, indeed," said Mom. "And they're lost. Tell them we're terribly sorry. Hey, kids, what was it that you are looking for?"

"A palace." Bridget said. "The Palace of Words. Have you seen it? It's supposed to be somewhere on this street."

"The palace—why, it's right there!" The old man pointed to a wall that ran the entire length of the street. "Come along, dear. Hurry!"

With that, the old couple vanished into the mist.

The kids turned to inspect the wall. On the other side of it was a palace, a genuine palace so large that somehow they had not noticed it.

Looking up at the enormous palace, Bridget felt as if she'd somehow stumbled into a fairy tale. "Wow," she said in wonder.

"Awesome," Barnaby agreed. "It fills up the whole block!"

"How do you suppose we get in there?" Beauregard asked. He thought even a cat as agile as he was might have trouble scaling that wall. It was at least eight feet high.

"Yoo-hoo!" Babette saw a shadowy figure in a window. "Hello? Could you let us in, please? We're looking for some spelling help!" The figure withdrew.

"You think anyone heard us?" Bridget asked.

Suddenly, a door in the wall popped open, and a man stepped out. To put it kindly, he was peculiar looking. He was just as tall and skinny as the old woman. The ends of his long pointed mustache stuck straight out like two paintbrushes. His nose was sharp and red, and his eyes were angry. On the top of his head was a flat helmet that looked something like a pie plate. At his side was a long sword in a sheath. Most surprising of all, he was wearing a suit of armor.

"Halt!" this amazing person yelled. "Who goes there?"

"Who are you?" Babette asked. She was so surprised to see the strange man that she forgot all her manners.

"What are you?" Barnaby repeated.

"I am Sir Pete, the Guard of Spelling. I know perfectly well who I am. What I don't know is who you are! And how dare you disturb the peace of the Palace?! I ought to cut off your heads!"

"I'm Barnaby. These are my friends, Babette, Beauregard, and Bridget. We are not disturbing anyone's peace—and we will thank you to keep that dangerous-looking sword in its sheath. Why, you could poke someone's eye out with that thing!"

"You better not cut off my head," Bridget said hotly.

"State your business," cried the Guard of Spelling, "or begone!" He put his hand on the hilt of his sword and frowned down at them so ferociously that Babette took a step backward. Unfortunately, the tremendously frightening effect the Guard intended to make was somewhat spoiled by the fact that his pie-plate helmet tipped forward and covered his eyes. Also, the man's sword came out of its sheath just far enough that the kids realized it was not a real sword—it was just a handle. The whole blade was missing!

The kids tried not to laugh.

Babette stepped forward. "We've come for a spelling lesson. We read about the Palace in the Yellow Pages. 'Everybody Welcome!' it said. I hope you are not guilty of false advertising. Our friend Beauregard here needs all the help he can get with his spelling. And to tell you the truth, I need a little help, too."

"A little?" snorted the Guard. He pushed his helmet back to the top of his head and folded his arms. "I will be the judge of that! Are you ready for your test?"

"Test? There's a test?" Beauregard frowned. "You mean a spelling test?" He absolutely hated tests, especially the spelling variety.

"Of course there's a test. I love giving tests. My test is wonderfully difficult. You have little chance of passing it." The Guard quickly eye-balled each of them up and down, making his assessment. "Obviously, all of you are bad spellers. Turn around and go away. Good-bye." The Guard stepped backward into the doorway and prepared to shut the door.

"Hey, wait a minute!" Barnaby said.

"We are not bad spellers," Bridget protested. "At least I'm not."

"Bridget is a great speller, sir," Babette said, "the best speller in her entire school. She's won contests!"

"Humph!" said Sir Pete.

"Go ahead, give us the test," Babette said. "You'll see."

"Since you are so bold," the Guard told Babette, "I will start with you." He gazed up at the sky and fingered the hilt of his sword. "Spell ASSISTANT."

"Assistant?" Babette realized it was one of the hard words, the kind where it is hard to remember how many Ss there are.

"You heard me. Spell ASSISTANT. I haven't all day."

Babette sounded the word out in her head. Uh — sis — tent. She was pretty sure it began with the letter 'a.'

"A," she said softly.

"Go on," the Guard commanded.

"A–S."

"You're doing great, Babette!" whispered Bridget.

Babette took a deep breath, "A–S–I–S–T–E–N–T."

Bridget groaned.

"Wrong! Completely and utterly wrong!" Sir Pete, the Guard of Spelling sounded downright pleased that Babette had made a mistake. "Next!" He glared at Barnaby. "You don't look especially bright. Do you want to forfeit? Do I even need to bother thinking up a word?"

Barnaby frowned stubbornly, "We'll see who's bright. What's the word?"

The Guard reached inside his armor and pulled out a piece of paper. He gave it a quick glance, then smiled. He put away the piece of paper, put his hands on his hips, and peered down his nose at Barnaby. "RESTAURANT. Spell it." The Guard smiled thinly and twirled one of the ends of his mustache. "If you can."

"Restaurant," Barnaby said. "Well, that's easy enough. It's a word I've seen a thousand times." "R–E–S," Barnaby hesitated.

To encourage him, Bridget gave Barnaby a grin and the thumbs-up sign.

"R–E–S–T–U–R–A–N–T."

Bridget quit grinning. Barnaby turned bright red.

"Wrong!" the Guard shouted, more pleased than ever. "Who's next?" He gazed down at Beauregard, who was trying to hide behind Barnaby. "You there, the cat—what's your name?"

"Beauregard." The cat knew he was the worst speller in the group. If Babette and Barnaby failed the test, then he didn't have a chance in the world. "I'm really not a good speller, sir. You needn't bother testing me, I'm sure."

The Guard was again staring at his piece of paper. "STOM-ACHACHE." He smiled to himself.

Bridget groaned. She knew that her friend the cat would never spell the word correctly. *Stomachache* is one of the hardest words to spell. Barnaby and Bridget smiled encouragingly at Beauregard. They didn't want to let him know they too thought he did not have a chance of spelling the difficult word correctly.

Beauregard closed his eyes. He remembered a TV commercial. It was a commercial for a fizzy pill that was good for an upset stomach. In big, thick, blue letters the word STOMACHACHE appeared, and the word grew until it filled the TV screen. Then the word vibrated and twisted and throbbed as if *it* had a stomachache!

"S–T–O," Beauregard said.

Babette sighed. He's gone wrong already, she thought, it's S–T–U.

Bridget knew that in fact Beauregard had started off correctly. The word *stomach* sounds as if it is spelled S–T–U–M–I–C–K, but really it starts out S–T–O. To give Beauregard good luck, she closed her eyes and crossed her fingers.

"S–T–O–M–A–C–H," Beauregard said.

"Oh," Babette murmured sadly, "poor Beauregard, he is really off."

Bridget opened her eyes. She could hardly believe Beauregard had spelled the first part of the word correctly. Of course, the cat would never spell "ache" correctly. "Ache" is one of the craziest words in the English language. Beauregard would say "A–K–E" or something.

"S–T–O–M–A–C–H," Beauregard squeezed shut his eyes until he could see the throbbing, vibrating, blue word exactly as it appeared in the TV commercial, "A–C–H–E!"

He opened his eyes. All three of his friends were staring at him in amazement.

"Oh, dear," the cat said. "Got it wrong, did I?"

"Humph!" the Guard said ferociously. "Correct!"

"Excuse me, sir. I thought you said...," began Beauregard, but he got no further because the three kids were jumping all around him, cheering and hugging him.

"Two wrong, one right," said the obviously irritated Guard. "Cease making all that racket, or I shall disqualify every one of you. You there, girl, whatever your name is."

"Her name is Bridget," Barnaby said, "and she's the best speller you've ever seen!"

Bridget beamed; she loved to be praised, especially by Barnaby.

"Give her the hardest word you've got," Barnaby said. "She loves a challenge. Don't you, Bridget?"

Bridget yanked down hard on her baseball cap. She sort of wished that Barnaby had kept his mouth shut about how much she liked a challenge.

The Guard folded up his list and put it away. "So you are a champion speller, are you? In that case, I have a very special question for you."

"Go on, big guy, lay it on me." Bridget winked at her friends.

"There are two words in the English language that are spelled without the letters A, E, I, O, or U. What are they?" The Guard folded his arms and smiled. He had an odd gleam in his eyes, as if he were up to no good.

His smile was so smug, so self-satisfied, that Barnaby thought he'd like to give the Guard a good, hard kick except he would probably hurt his toe on that armor.

"Gypsy," Bridget said. "G–Y–P–S–Y. That's one."

Barnaby, Babette, and Beauregard blinked in amazement, then burst into a loud cheer. "Go, Bridget, go!"

Bridget looked down at the toe of her tennis shoe. She closed her eyes and crossed the fingers of her right hand. Then she crossed the fingers of her left hand.

The Guard looked at his watch. "You have one minute."

Bridget's jaws moved up and down as she chewed her gum. Barnaby thought he could almost see the wheels turning in his friend's brain as she tried to come up with the other word that has no vowels.

"Time's up," cried the Guard. "What's the answer?"

Bridget opened her eyes and uncrossed her fingers. She quit chewing her gum.

"Tell him, Bridget!" said Barnaby.

Bridget turned red. "Um, uh,…I don't even think there is another word that's spelled without an A, E, I, O, or U." Just as she said this out loud Bridget felt something was wrong, she asked herself, "Are there really only two words spelled without a vowel?" She sensed that something was not right with this Guard of Spelling. "Is he up to no good?" She asked herself.

"Ha!" the Guard smiled happily. "I thought so! You there, cat, come with me." He turned on his heel and went back into the doorway. Beauregard scurried after him.

"Hey," Barnaby said. He took a step toward the door. "At least tell us the answer!"

Bam!

The Guard of Spelling slammed shut the door in Barnaby's face. *Click.* Barnaby heard the lock turn. He turned to look at Babette and Bridget. It seemed unbelievable. Their friend Beauregard had deserted them just like that, and they were locked out of the Palace of Words!

"Now, what are we going to do?" Bridget asked.

"Hey, kids," a voice called. "Up here!"

They looked up.

In the Palace's nearest tower, a window opened. A slender arm emerged and tossed something out. It fell through the air and landed, *clink*, on the sidewalk not far from the kids. The arm withdrew, and the window closed with a bang.

"What is it?" Bridget said. She wondered if the Palace really might contain a princess in distress. That arm had looked like a girl's arm.

Babette bent down. She unwrapped a carefully folded package. "Why, it's a key!" She held out a large golden key. "And a note."

"What's it say?" Barnaby demanded. "Don't keep us in suspense."

"Rhythm."

"What?"

Bridget slapped herself hard on the forehead. "Of course, rhythm!"

"Maybe I'm dumb," Barnaby said, "but I don't get it."

"Rhythm," Bridget said. "R–H–Y–T–H–M. It's the other word besides 'gypsy' that doesn't have an A, E, I, O, or U!"

"Wow," Barnaby said, scratching his bushy head of hair. "Who threw that note?"

Babette aimed the golden key at the large keyhole in the door and walked straight toward it. She turned the key in the lock and the door sprang open. "Should we go in?" she asked a little uneasily.

The two other kids looked at one another.

"It's almost like trespassing," Barnaby nervously responded.

Bridget grinned at him, "So stay right here if you're scared. We'll tell you all about it when we get back!" With a quick tug, she adjusted her baseball cap the way she liked it and ran through the door.

Babette grinned and followed her friend. Barnaby wondered if this was wise, but he couldn't let Babette and Bridget go by themselves. He followed after them. After all, someone had tossed down a key. In a way, that was an outright invitation.

The moment Barnaby went through the door, it snapped shut behind him and automatically locked. He tried to open it, but the door would not budge. "I guess we've got no choice," he said.

Inside the wall, a narrow path led straight to the back of the Palace. There was a large open window and a tall, thin, green door with all the letters of the alphabet painted on it.

"Do you think it's locked?" Babette wondered. "Should I try the doorknob?"

"Hey, listen," Bridget said. "Hear that sound? What is that?"

All three of them listened carefully.

"It's clicking," Barnaby said. "It sounds like—"

"Like nails on a tile floor," Bridget said. "You know, like a dog's toenails!"

"Hey! Watch out!" Barnaby yelled.

A huge, red dog leapt right out of the open window and bounded toward them! It was an enormous beast that was the size of a horse! Before any of them could think what to do, the giant red dog grabbed hold of Barnaby's shirt, picked him up, and bounded back into the Palace carrying Barnaby in its mouth!

Babette and Bridget stared at the open window, then stared at each other.

"Come on!" Bridget yelled. She dove into the open window. Babette dove right in after her.

Exercises for Chapter 2

Although we hate to interrupt the story, this is a good place to stick in some more advice about learning to spell. Take another look at the "hard" words the Guard of Spelling used to stump Barnaby, Bridget, and Babette. If you can learn to spell these five words (STOMACHACHE, ASSISTANT, RESTAURANT, GYPSY, and RHYTHM), you can learn to spell anything! Let's get started by seeing if you can learn them.

STOMACHACHE—This word is hard because it does you no good to sound it out. It sounds as if it should be spelled STUMICK AKE, but if you spell it that way, it would definitely be a mistake.

Here is a good method for learning to spell a new word:

1. Pronounce the word loudly while you look at it carefully. STOMACHACHE.

2. Look carefully at the parts of the word. STOMACH–ACHE.

3. While looking at the letters, say them out loud. S–T–O–M–A–C–H–A–C–H–E. Some spellers love to trace out each letter in the air with their finger as they spell; some even like to point their chin out and trace the letters that way.

4. Close your eyes. Visualize the word and spell it to yourself. Open your eyes and check to see if you made any mistakes.

5. Now, write the word down on a piece of paper.

6. Check your spelling attempt. How'd you do?

If you spelled STOMACHACHE perfectly, congratulations! Now, write it down five more times just for practice!

Did you make a mistake? Which *part* of the word did you miss? Most spellers only make a mistake in one part of a word. Underline that part. Trace the letters again. Close your eyes and visualize the word—*especially the part you missed.* Check to see if you are right. Then write it down. Write it down five more times.

Use this same system for learning to spell the other four hard words.

ASSISTANT is hard for two reasons. It has all those Ss—three of them. Its last syllable could be spelled ANT or ENT. Try to remember, ASSISTANT has a pair of Ss, then an S all by its lonesome. It ends with ANT.

RESTAURANT. For most spellers, the hard part of this word is the middle, the AU. It is easy to make a mistake and think the AU must go in the last syllable. Start with REST—then the AU—then RANT. Notice there is an ANT in RESTAURANT.

Some spellers like to think up *easy-to-remember pictures*. Think of a restaurant counter crawling with ANTs! Someone is RESTing on top of the counter—on his "middle" the ants have lined up and spelled out the letters AU!

GYPSY and RHYTHM are tricky words because they don't contain the normal vowels (A, E, I, O, and/or U). The key is to practice them over and over until, when misspelled, the words actually look strange to you.

Work on all five of these words until you learn them perfectly—then give yourself a treat. Call up a good friend, eat some ice cream, or go play with your dog. You deserve it!

Like we said, if you can learn to spell the Guard of Spelling's five hard words, you can learn to spell *any* word!

Chapter 3:
I Before *E* Except After *C*

When you know a word contains an *I* and an *E*, remember this rule: *I* BEFORE *E* EXCEPT AFTER *C.*

The Guard of Spelling escorted Beauregard through the Palace that seemed to consist of miles of hallways. Each corridor was lined in carpet so deep and thick that, as they walked, they made not the slightest sound.

"Sir Pete, if you don't mind my asking," the cat asked, "where are we going?" He wondered what had become of Barnaby, Bridget, and Babette and hoped they weren't mad at him for abandoning them, but what else could he do? After all, he was a cat, and cats are famous for their curiosity. He couldn't miss an opportunity to explore the palace.

Sir Pete did not answer Beauregard's question. Instead, he led Beauregard up a flight of stairs and down a corridor and through a room and down another flight of stairs. They turned left, then right, then left again—until at last Beauregard was so turned around, he hadn't the vaguest idea where he was.

"Here we are!" said the Guard of Spelling. He rapped on a door, then stood as straight and tall as he could.

From inside the door, a high-pitched, angry voice cried, "Who is it? Who's there? I'm busy!"

"It is I, Sir Pete, the Guard of Spelling!"

At once, the voice on the other side of the door changed. It became soft and sweet. "Come in, Sir Pete. You are very welcome, I'm sure!"

The Guard threw open the door. "Follow me," he told Beauregard. "Mind your manners."

Seated in a soft armchair in the middle of the room was a well-dressed woman. She was tall and skinny. Her hair was in a bun at the back of her head. She had long bony fingers and a long sharp nose with a small pair of glasses perched on the end of it. In her lap was a pillowcase and some sewing equipment. She was embroidering.

Smiling coyly and fluttering her eyelashes, the woman held up the pillowcase. "What do you think, Sir Pete? I've just finished!"

The Guard of Spelling sniffed and bent over to inspect the pillowcase. "Very nice, your Highness."

On the pillowcase was stitched: *I* Before *E* Except After *C*.

The Guard straightened up, cleared his throat and said, "Your Highness, we have a visitor. A cat."

She looked doubtfully at the cat.

"He is an excellent speller, your Highness. I've tested him."

The woman arched a thin eyebrow. "Is he? A beast who spells! Come here into the light, kitty."

Although Beauregard did not like to be called a beast, and absolutely hated anyone calling him "kitty," he obediently stepped forward into the light.

"Cat, this is her Highness, the Duchess of Rules. If you know what's good for you, serve her well. Your Highness, I'll leave you two together. I have business elsewhere." The Guard closed the door and departed.

"I'd hoped he'd stay longer." The Duchess laid down her sewing. "Sir Pete is always in such a terrible hurry. He's the Guard of Spelling, you know, and that job is terribly important." She peered intently down at Beauregard through her round glasses. "Why, without him the entire language would soon disintegrate into chaos. Sir Pete is an amazingly fine speller. Did you know he's only misspelled one word in his entire career as the Guard of Spelling? It's the truth. He consistently misspells the word MARRIAGE. He neglects to put the *I* in it. Isn't that curious?" She looked rather thoughtful.

Beauregard tried to think of something nice to say. "What a nice pillowcase. Did you do all that beautiful embroidery yourself?"

She held it up. "It is beautiful, isn't it?"

Beauregard read aloud the words embroidered on the case, "*I* Before *E* Except After *C*." He didn't have the slightest idea what the mysterious sentence could mean.

The Duchess took off her glasses and wiped a tear from her left eye. "Isn't that a gorgeous rule? Isn't it poetry?" She put her glasses back on.

Beauregard wiggled his whiskers. "Er, if I might ask a question?"

"Please, do."

"What does it mean? *I* Before *E*. What does that mean exactly?"

"Why, it's a spelling rule. When you know a word contains an *I* and an *E*, and you don't know which comes first, you remember this perfectly lovely rule. *I* Before *E* Except After *C*. All rules are beautiful. Don't you just love them?"

In fact, Beauregard was rather fond of bending and breaking rules, but he did not think it wise to say so. He looked around the room. On its walls were many other examples of the Duchess's skill at embroidery.

"Would you like to look at my little works of art?" The Duchess rose to her feet. "Look at this one—done just last week." She pointed to an embroidered square hanging on the wall.

"No Eglish Words End In *V*," Beauregard read.

"You recited that rule with such expression!" the Duchess exclaimed. She laid her hand on her heart. "Why, you must be a very good speller, indeed!"

Because Beauregard was nothing of the kind, he squirmed with embarrassment. Should he confess?

"This one," the Duchess said, "is a darling." She tapped another embroidered square of cloth.

The Letter *Q* is Always Followed by *U*.

"And here's another old favorite."

"Proper Nouns Begin With Capitals," Beauregard read.

"I simply adore rules, don't you? All rules are perfectly delicious, but my very favorite of all is this one." She held up the embroidered pillowcase again. "*I* Before *E* Except After *C*. Why, it's music!"

Beauregard asked, "Do you think if someone—a bad speller, let's say—memorized all these rules, would he turn into a good speller?" He wiggled his whiskers hopefully.

The Duchess stiffened her back; a spot of pink appeared in each of her cheeks.

"There are no exceptions, are there? I mean, a rule is a rule." Beauregard was about to go on when he suddenly noticed that the Duchess looked as if she'd swallowed a fish bone. She gasped. She waved her fists in the air.

"The French!" the Duchess cried. "Oh, how I hate them. It's their fault! And Latin. Why did everyone have to bother with Latin?! And the dictionary makers! Oh, dear!" She sat down and fanned herself with her hand. "How do I look? Have I gone red in the face? I have to watch my blood pressure."

"Take a deep breath," Beauregard advised. "That's what I do when I get mad. Then I count to ten and swish my tail."

"It all happened so long ago, centuries ago. I shouldn't get angry about what can't be helped—but I do!"

"Was it something about rules? Exceptions?"

"If only our lovely English language had been built on top of simple and sensible rules."

"It wasn't?"

"It was built up helter-skelter, without any real plan. Centuries ago, the French came to England. They invaded the island

and took over. Before long, French words were everywhere. And ridiculous French expressions—and spellings! Then everyone grew terribly fond of Latin. People care very little about Latin today, but in the eighteenth century educated people were perfectly mad about the language."

"And that affected English?"

"It certainly did. Oh, it had an awful effect. But there it is— one thing or another is always making an impact on the English language. The English people conquered lands all over the world, and in every new country they learned new words. That is why our language is so big and so complicated and so terribly difficult. I blame the dictionary makers, you know. They could have cleaned everything up. They could have laid down a few simple rules and eliminated any and all inconsistencies. But you know what they did? They would take a word that was pronounced a certain way in one place, in northern England for example, and link it to the way the word was spelled somewhere else, in London for example. Then, just to make more trouble, they would list six different meanings for one word!"

"That is confusing," Beauregard agreed. "No wonder, I'm— er, I mean, some people are bad spellers."

"And the sounds! Don't get me started. Some sounds may be spelled five different ways. Some letters may be pronounced three different ways! No wonder so many people can't spell." She lowered her voice. "What some people believe is that we need a revolution."

Noticing the Duchess was starting to turn a little pink again, Beauregard tried to calm her down by whispering, "A revolution?"

"Rationalized spelling!" The Duchess reached under her armchair. She reared up suddenly. "Hark! Listen! Do you hear anything?"

Beauregard listened. "No, nothing."

The Duchess pulled a thick manuscript out from under her chair and held it out to Beauregard. "This is top secret. It is a Dictionary of Rationalized Spelling. Want to take a look?"

Beauregard took the manuscript and gazed doubtfully down at the huge wad of paper.

"We must lower our voices. The Guard may return at any moment. He doesn't approve, you know. He's so old-fashioned!"

Beauregard read the first page of the great mass of paper.

"I got it off the Internet, and it doesn't appear to have an author. I believe it's really just a version of something Mark Twain wrote a long time ago," the Duchess explained. "What do you think? It's just a little radical perhaps."

Beauregard read:

"English spelling is much too difficult. Consider words like these: see and sea, here and hear, to and too and two. Why should we put up with all these difficulties? What we need is a Revolution! Listen to our secret plan. First, we will use 's' instead of the soft 'c.' Sertainly, sivil servants in all sities will resieve this news with joy. The hard 'c' would then be replased by 'k' sinse both letters are pronounsed alike. This will not only klear up konfusion in the minds of klerikal workers, but typewriters and keyboards kould be made with one less letter. For our second step, we'll announce that the troublesome 'ph' will be written 'f.' This will make words like 'fotograf' much shorter to write. In the third stage, publik akseptanse of the new spelling kan be expekted to reach the stage where more komplikated changes are possible. We will enkourage the removal of double letters which have always ben a deterent to akurate speling. We al agre that the horible mes of silent 'e's' in the languag is disgrasful. Therefor, we kould drop thes and kontinu to read and writ as though nothing had hapend. When al thes changs ar akseptd, people will be reseptiv to steps such as replasing 'th' by 'z.' Perhaps zen ze funktion of 'w' kould be taken on by 'v,' vitsh is, after al, half a 'w.' Finaly, ze unesesary 'o' kuld be dropd from vords kontaining 'ou.' Similar arguments vud of kors be aplid to ozer kombinations of leters. Ve vud eventuli hav a reli sensibl riten stil! Zer vud be no more trubls with speling and evrion vud fin it ezi tu understan esh ozer!"

"My goodness," Beauregard said when he finished. "I really don't know what to say. Do you think changes like these are really possible?"

"Isn't rationalized spelling wonderful? Rules, rules, rules—and with no exceptions!" The Duchess had turned bright red. Blazing with dangerous excitement, she strode around the room.

Beauregard was just about to say that, although an English language made entirely out of rules seemed quite a bit easier to spell, it might be very difficult to get everyone to go along with it. Rationalized spelling just looked too ridiculous on the page. And think of the millions of books that would have to be entirely rewritten!

Knock-knock. Knock-knock-knock! "Are you all right in there, your Highness?"

It was the voice of the Guard of Spelling.

The Duchess leapt straight up into the air. She rushed to Beauregard, grabbed the big Dictionary of Rationalized Spelling out of his paws and stuffed it back under her armchair.

"Yes, Sir Pete, what is it?" Her long thin fingers patted her bun of hair. "Come in, please." She adjusted her glasses.

The Guard of Spelling threw open the door and strode into the room. "There's been a serious disturbance, your Highness. Are you all right?"

"My goodness, what's happened?"

"Thieves, your Highness. Three trespassers have invaded the Palace!"

The Duchess let out a little shriek as if she thought some of the thieves might be right in her sitting room.

"No need to be alarmed. The trespassers have been captured. They are being held in the dungeon."

"Thank goodness!" exclaimed the Duchess. "Trespassers! In the Palace! Why, I've never heard of anything so awful. How brave of you, how wonderful of you to capture them!"

Beauregard motioned wildly at the Duchess until he caught her eye.

"Yes, what is it, kitty?" the Duchess asked.

Beauregard ran up to her side and whispered into her ear.

"All right, I'll ask him," the Duchess told Beauregard. "Excuse me, sir, we were wondering—did you say you caught *three* trespassers?"

The Guard of Spelling twirled his mustache. "Yes, ma'am, three." His fingers played with the handle of his sword. "Two females and a male."

Beauregard made a little yelp, then whispered again into the Duchess's ear.

"I wonder, Sir Pete, perhaps you might show us the three prisoners. Kitty here would like to see the criminals."

The Guard twirled his mustache, "Hmm. Then come with me!"

Beauregard trotted to keep up with the Duchess and the Guard. They both had long legs and took rapid strides.

Beauregard had no doubt the three "trespassers" were his friends Babette, Bridget, and Barnaby. Somehow the kids had found a way to enter the Palace!

The Guard led them down a corridor to an elevator.

As the elevator began its descent, the Guard said, "I'm not surprised this creature wants to see the prisoners. They are friends of his."

"No!" The Duchess looked uneasily at Beauregard. "He has criminals for friends?" She moved a little closer to the Guard and a little farther from Beauregard.

"His friends are worse than criminals; they are bad spellers!"

The Duchess gasped. She moved around the back of the elevator so that the Guard stood between her and Beauregard. "I...I had no idea," she stuttered, the pink reappearing in her cheeks.

"In fact," the Guard said, "I've begun to wonder if this cat is in fact a good speller at all."

"But of course I am," Beauregard cried befordàáe could stop himself.

Sir Pete smiled. "Why don't you entertain us, cat, by spelling a few words?"

Beauregard wiggled his long whiskers and lashed his tail, "Oh, I don't think the Duchess wants me to…"

"Spell 'friend,' Kitty," said the Duchess.

Beauregard thought desperately. Could the word be spelled F–R–E–N–D? No, that was wrong. It had an 'i' in it somewhere. He was about to spell it F–R–E–I–N–D, when he remembered the rule the Duchess had taught him: I Before E Except After C. Beauregard smiled and with great confidence spelled the word out loud. "F–R–I–E–N–D!" When finished, he took a little bow.

"Very good!" The Duchess clapped her hands. "You see, Sir Pete, he is a good speller after all. *I* Before *E* Except After *C*— isn't it a wonderful rule, kitty?"

The Guard of Spelling cleared his throat. He pulled hard on his left mustache, then equally hard on his right mustache. "Spell 'weird,' cat."

The Duchess's color started to heighten from pink to red.

"Weird?" Beauregard said. Brushing the rear of the elevator, his tail whisked nervously from side to side.

"Weird." The Guard smiled faintly.

"Really, sir," said the Duchess, "I don't think that is a very nice word, is it? Could he spell another one? 'Believe' perhaps?"

"Go on," the Guard said sternly. "Weird!"

Remembering the Duchess's favorite rule, Beauregard spelled the word. "W–I–E–R–D."

"Wrong!" the Guard cried triumphantly.

The elevator ground to a stop and its door began to open. The Guard reached down and took a firm hold of Beauregard's collar, "Here we are! Watch your step, your Highness."

Beauregard let out a forlorn meow.

"I think you," the Guard gave Beauregard a hard shake, "can join your friends—in the Dungeon for Bad Spellers!"

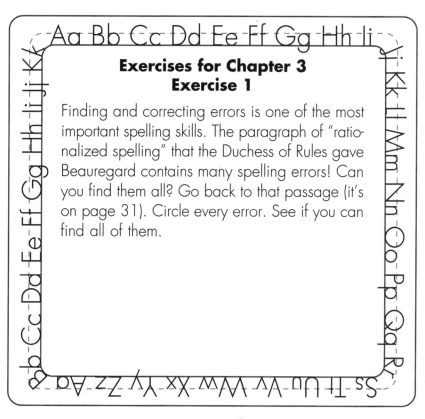

Exercises for Chapter 3
Exercise 1

Finding and correcting errors is one of the most important spelling skills. The paragraph of "rationalized spelling" that the Duchess of Rules gave Beauregard contains many spelling errors! Can you find them all? Go back to that passage (it's on page 31). Circle every error. See if you can find all of them.

see pages 247–248 for answers

Exercise 2

The paragraph of "rationalized spelling" is a good illustration of words that are hard to spell because they contain certain special combinations of letters. Here is a list of some words that are typically hard to spell. Look at each misspelled word. Figure out what is wrong with it, then write the correct spelling of the word right beside it.

Soft Cs (the usual mistake is to put an S instead of the C)

sertainly

sivil

sities

resieve

replased

sinse

pronounsed

akseptanse

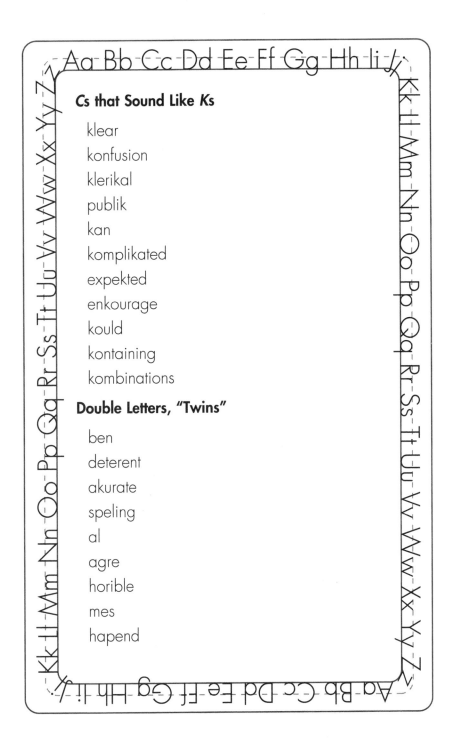

Cs that Sound Like *K*s

klear

konfusion

klerikal

publik

kan

komplikated

expekted

enkourage

kould

kontaining

kombinations

Double Letters, "Twins"

ben

deterent

akurate

speling

al

agre

horible

mes

hapend

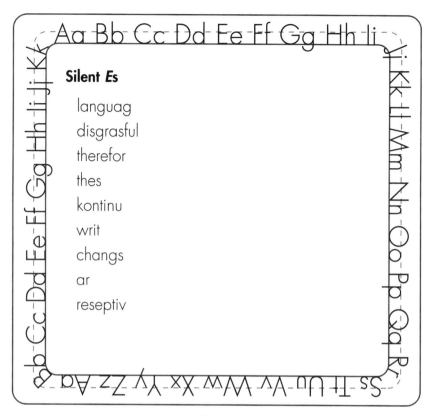

Silent *Es*

languag

disgrasful

therefor

thes

kontinu

writ

changs

ar

reseptiv

see pages 248–249 for answers

Exercise 3

I Before *E* Except After *C*: Some Exceptions to the Rule

The Duchess's favorite rule is a pretty useful—most of the time! But as Beauregard found out, there are definitely some exceptions. Here is a list of some common words where *I* does *not* come before *E*. See if you can learn to spell these tricky rule-breakers.

> leisure
>
> neighbor (when the EI combination is pronounced so it sounds like A, it is spelled EI)
>
> neither
>
> seize
>
> their
>
> weird (some spellers get this one right by remembering the little saying, "Weird is WEIRD.")
>
> weigh (this one is like NEIGHBOR—the EI combination sounds like A)

Chapter 4:
The Dungeon for Bad Spellers

Even so-called bad spellers can learn tricks to help them spell better.

The hound carried Barnaby in his teeth. The big beast trotted along as if he was used to carrying kids in his mouth. "Hey!" Barnaby yelped.

Bridget and Babette tumbled into the open window. They landed on a tile floor and jumped to their feet. "Did you see where they went?" asked Babette.

"This way!" yelled Bridget.

The dog ran into a stairwell and leapt down several flights of stairs. Babette and Bridget ran down the steps after it, but the dog was much faster than they were. When they got to the bottom of the last flight of stairs, they seemed to be in some sort of deep basement underneath the Palace.

"Gee, where'd they go? Did you see?" Bridget asked.

"There's an open door!" Babette pointed. "It must have taken Barnaby in there." She took off her sunglasses in order to be able to see better in the dim light.

"You don't think that beast could be, you know...dangerous?" Bridget asked, her voice quavering.

"Hey, Barnaby!" she yelled. "You down here?"

"In here! Help! I'm in here!"

Bridget and Babette ran through the open door into a large room full of tables. "Barnaby! Where are you?" yelled Bridget.

"Back here! He's got me trapped in this corner!"

The huge dog had let go of Barnaby. His face was flushed and his shirt was a little torn, but otherwise Barnaby seemed unharmed. He was trapped in a corner all right—by a dog the size of a horse.

The enormous dog had his head turned sideways and was looking at Bridget. He licked his chops.

"Nice doggy," Bridget said uneasily.

Before any of them could think what to do next, the dog bounded into the air. With three big leaps, it rushed past them and out the open door.

"Hey!" Bridget yelled.

Using his nose, the dog pushed the door shut with a loud bang!

Bridget tried the knob. "I knew it," she said. "We're locked in! It's like the dog got us down here on purpose!"

"All I know," Babette said, "is that I'm glad we're rid of it. What a monster! I'm still trembling!"

"So you met Woof, did you?" a voice said.

They whirled around and stared at a very tall girl. She had a large nose and a funny mouth that was screwed sideways in a semi-grin. Her hair was tied in a fat braid that hung straight down her back. The tall girl was sprawled on a long sofa and held a book in her hand.

"Wolf?" Bridget said. "That was a real wolf?"

"Not Wolf," the girl put down her book and sat up. "Woof. That's what I call him anyway. Woof-Woof the Killer."

"Woof-Woof scared me half to death," Bridget admitted.

"Did you say—killer?" Barnaby asked.

"You're lucky to be alive," the tall girl said. "Woof ate a couple bad spellers this morning. I guess that's why he let you go. He's not hungry. Not yet anyway." She stuck out her hand. "Hi, my name's Beth."

"Ate them?" Babette asked. She shook the tall girl's hand.

"Woof hates bad spellers."

Bridget, Barnaby, and Babette introduced themselves.

"But that's terrible!" Babette cried. "He *ate* them?!"

"How'd you guys get here anyway? Just wander in off the street?"

Barnaby explained how they'd found the ad for the Palace of Words in the Yellow Pages. "We came here to get some help for our friend Beauregard. He's a bad speller. We thought we'd be welcome."

"Typical," the tall girl gave her braid a hard tug. "That's how the King and Queen lure bad spellers to this Palace. They just *hate* bad spellers."

"They lure people here?" Babette said. "But that's awful! That's worse than awful!"

"Woof would have gobbled me up a long time ago, except I got smart and fed him some pork chops. That beast is nuts about pork chops. He's been my pal ever since."

Barnaby, Bridget, and Babette exchanged glances. Could all this be true? A dog who ate bad spellers? A king and queen who lured kids to this dangerous Palace?

"So what are you guys in for?" The tall girl stood to her feet. She was taller than any of them; she stood at almost six feet tall. "This is the Dungeon for Bad Spellers, so I figure you guys must have misspelled something."

"You got that right!" Bridget explained how Barnaby had misspelled RESTAURANT, and Babette had misspelled ASSIS-TANT.

"What'd you misspell?" Beth asked her. "Something hard I bet. The Guard is really great at coming up with words that are practically impossible to spell. You know what I think? He gets a sick pleasure out of causing kids to make mistakes."

"I didn't misspell anything. I'm a champion speller. I just forgot that RHYTHM was the only other word in the English language besides GYPSY that doesn't contain a normal vowel." Bridget pulled off her baseball cap, banged it against her knee, and put it back on. "It was a trick question!"

"BY," the tall girl said. "And MY."

"What?" said Barnaby.

The tall girl added, "And WHY."

Bridget blushed and smacked herself on the head. How could she have forgotten that there were more words—simple, common words too—that did not use A, E, I, O, or U?

"Well, if you're in here," the tall girl said, "they figure you're a bad speller, that's all I know. This is the Dungeon for Bad Spellers." The tall girl played with her thick braid. "I get tossed in here all the time."

Barnaby and the others looked around at the Dungeon.

"This is a dungeon?" Babette asked.

"It doesn't exactly seem like a normal dungeon," Barnaby said. "I mean, where are the torture devices and the iron rings in the walls?"

Bridget said, "It looks like... like a classroom!"

The Dungeon for Bad Spellers did indeed look like a class-room. It had comfortable furniture, long tables surrounded by chairs, and blackboards complete with chalk. On one wall were shelves of books.

"Check out the wallpaper," Bridget said.

"Why, it is covered with words!" Babette said. "Hundreds of thousands of words!"

It seemed amazing, but the walls of the Dungeon were completely covered with words and their definitions.

"It's a dictionary!" Barnaby said. "It's the pages of a dictionary." It seemed amazing, but someone had carefully torn out all the pages of a dictionary and wallpapered the Dungeon with them.

"My brother Biff did it," Beth explained.

"You have a brother?" Barnaby asked. "Here?" He looked around the Dungeon, but they seemed to be alone.

"Not here. They've got Biff locked in the tower. The King threw a dictionary at him and told him he had to memorize all the words. Can you believe it?"

Stunned, Barnaby said slowly, "All...the...words... in...the...dictionary?!" He could hardly believe it. How could anyone possibly memorize all the words in the dictionary?

"Biff pasted the pages on these walls, but I don't think it helped that much. It's pretty sad all right." Beth sighed heavily and gave her braid a tug. "I'm gonna miss him."

Babette stood directly in front of the tall girl and looked up at her, "What do you mean, 'miss him?'"

"Unless he has all those words down letter-perfect, he's to be executed at dawn."

"All the words in the dictionary!" Barnaby yelled. "Or death? You can't be serious!"

"Not all of the words," Beth said. She walked over to a chalkboard and tapped a piece of paper taped to it with her index finger. "Just these words. Biff has to know how to spell all of them. The King and Queen are giving him a test in the morning. He has to get all of them right—or else." She drew her finger across her throat.

Barnaby, Bridget, and Babette ran forward to peer at the list. It was entitled "Fiendishly Hard Words."

"Wow, there's a lot of them," Babette said.

"Fifty-five," Beth replied. "And he has to get every one of them right. It's a list of the words junior high kids are most likely to misspell."

They all heard a noise as if someone was at the door to the Dungeon.

"Hey, did you guys hear something?" Bridget asked.

A key rattled in the lock. The door to the dungeon was flung open and someone entered the room.

Bridget smacked herself on the forehead, "Where have you been?!"

There in the doorway, looking a little frightened, stood Beauregard!

Exercise for Chapter 4

Fiendishly Hard Words

Frequently Misspelled Words—The Top 55 for Junior High Kids (listed in order of frequency of misspelling).

These are the words that junior high students are most likely to misspell in their ordinary writing. Your exercise for Chapter 4 is this: Get a pal or a parent to give you this test. Have them read each word out loud and use it in a sentence. After they read each word to you, try to spell it, writing your answers on a pad of paper. See how many you can get right. Do you think you can help Beth's brother Biff learn to spell all these words before dawn?

1. there

2. a lot

3. too

4. their

5. that's

6. it's

7. because

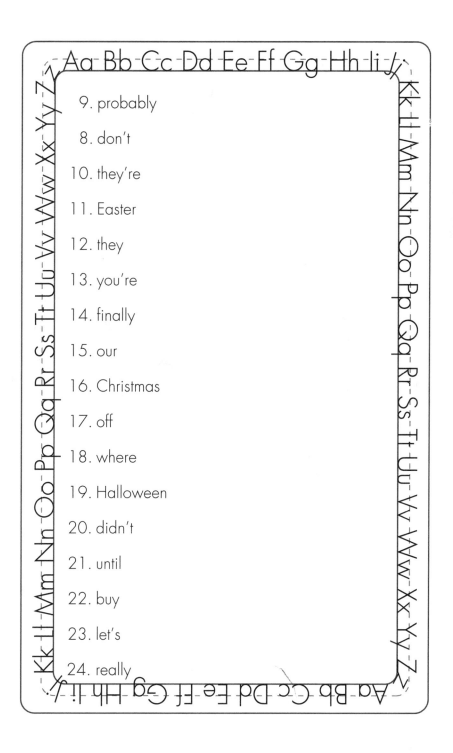

9. probably

8. don't

10. they're

11. Easter

12. they

13. you're

14. finally

15. our

16. Christmas

17. off

18. where

19. Halloween

20. didn't

21. until

22. buy

23. let's

24. really

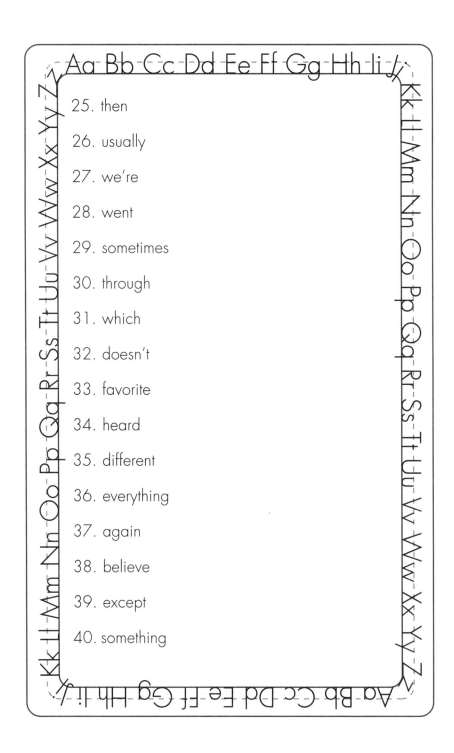

25. then

26. usually

27. we're

28. went

29. sometimes

30. through

31. which

32. doesn't

33. favorite

34. heard

35. different

36. everything

37. again

38. believe

39. except

40. something

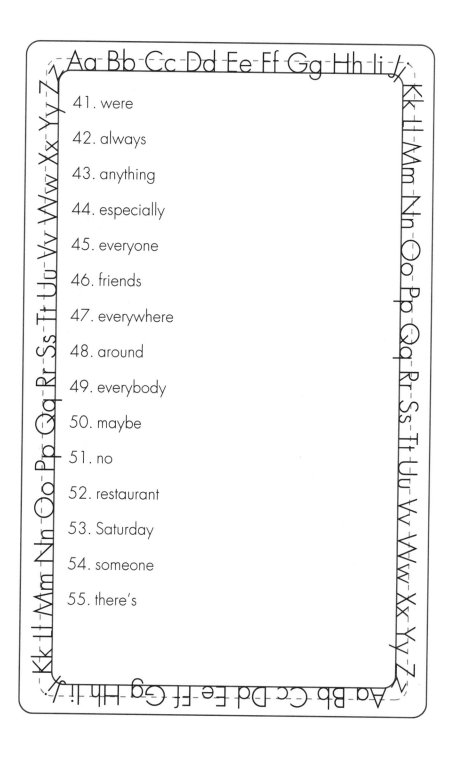

41. were

42. always

43. anything

44. especially

45. everyone

46. friends

47. everywhere

48. around

49. everybody

50. maybe

51. no

52. restaurant

53. Saturday

54. someone

55. there's

Learn to spell just one word from the "Fiendishly Hard Words" list and you've already become a better speller!

Chapter 5:
The Trapdoor Spelling Test

Name something you hang on a wall that tells you what day of the month it is. Read ahead to see if you spelled it correctly!

The Guard of Spelling tossed Beauregard into the Dungeon and slammed the door shut. Beauregard looked at his friends and shrugged. "They caught me," he explained. "The Guard figured out that I am the world's worst speller. He's not as dumb as he looks."

It took awhile for the kids and Beauregard to get caught up on their adventures. Beauregard told Barnaby, Bridget, and Babette all about his meeting with the Duchess of Rules. He was just about to tell them about how the Guard of Spelling had discovered that he was in fact a poor speller by tricking him with the rule-breaking word WEIRD, when suddenly he stood up on his hind legs and sniffed. "I smell something." Beauregard sniffed the air again. "A disgusting aroma. A putrid smell. The worst stench in the entire world!" His tail lashed, and his hair stood on end. "Dog! I smell dog!" Beauregard looked accusingly at Barnaby. "My friend, you smell of canine. I hate to say it, but you smell as if one of those foul-breathed, fang-toothed monsters has," Beauregard squirmed in disgust, "licked you!"

"Barnaby was attacked by a dog!" Babette said. "A perfect monster. He was practically killed by a gigantic beast."

Bridget said, "Go on, Barnaby, tell him!"

Barnaby told Beauregard how the huge dog named Woof had grabbed him and carried him down several flights of stairs to this dungeon. He was just about to tell more, when Beth cleared her throat.

"Is no one going to introduce me?" she asked, perturbed.

Bridget hit herself in the forehead. "Wow. I really forgot my manners. Beauregard, this is Beth." She pointed at the tall girl. "Oh, wow, I can't believe I forgot. Beauregard, we have to help Beth. Her brother needs to learn how to spell—and fast."

Babette explained that Beth's brother Biff was being held captive in the Palace Tower. Barnaby showed Beauregard the long list of Fiendishly Hard Words.

"It's a list of words junior high kids frequently mess up," Bridget explained. "If he flunks his spelling test, tomorrow at dawn..." she swallowed.

"...they're going to execute him!" Barnaby yelled.

"Jeepers," said the cat, "why that's..." his tail lashed; his whiskers wiggled. "I don't even have words to describe how truly bad that is. Why, we must save the boy at once. What are we waiting for? Where is this tower?"

"*Hel*-lo," Bridget said sarcastically. "Earth to Beauregard. We're locked in a dungeon. We can't even help ourselves. How do you suggest we rescue this kid?"

Babette and Barnaby looked dejected. Somehow they had to save Biff, they couldn't let someone be executed just because he couldn't spell Fiendishly Hard Words.

Beauregard looked again at the list of fifty-five difficult spelling words and felt lucky that he didn't have to spell them all. Then he felt angry. It just wasn't right! What kind of terrible place was this palace?

"We've got to bust out of here," Barnaby said.

"Yeah," Bridget agreed, "but how?"

"Well," Beth said.

"Yes?" Barnaby asked.

The tall girl tugged on her braid. "There is one way out of here. I just didn't want to mention it on account of the danger." Beth pointed toward a wall. "See that?"

On one wall of the Dungeon, not far from a blackboard at about eye-level, a small loudspeaker was embedded into the wall. Beside it was a red button about the size of a dime.

"What's that for?" Barnaby walked over to the red button. "Should I press it?"

"Watch where you're standing," Beth said. On the floor, in front of the speaker and the red button, was a big black square. It was impossible to touch the button without standing on the black square. Barnaby was standing right in the middle of it.

"It's a trapdoor," Beth explained. "You stand on the black square and push the button. After a second, you will hear a word come out of that wall speaker, which you have to spell within ten seconds."

"What happens if you spell it incorrectly?" Barnaby said uneasily.

"Nothing. Not one thing. It's when you spell it right that something happens."

"What?" Barnaby stepped back from the big black square.

"The trapdoor falls open and you're gone, that's what." She grinned. "Go on and push it if you're not afraid."

"Gone?" Bridget chewed her bubble gum rapidly. "What do you mean gone? Gone where?"

"Nobody knows, not for sure. Some kids say it leads directly to a roaring furnace."

"A furnace!" Babette cried.

"Others say it leads all the way to China."

"Oh, come on," Barnaby adjusted his glasses, "that's impossible—a hole clear through the center of the earth? That's ridiculous. You can't expect us to believe that."

"If you're so curious, go ahead and push the red button."

"But maybe it's a way out of here," Bridget said. "Maybe it leads to some place good."

"It could," Beth tugged her braid. "Then again it could lead straight to disaster. I've never tried it, so I can't say."

"That trapdoor is the only way out of here," Barnaby declared. "I'm going to push it. I mean, think about it. If you get into this dungeon by misspelling a word, doesn't it make sense that you can get out by spelling a word right?" Before anyone could object, Barnaby reached out and gave the red button a hard jab with his index finger.

The speaker crackled with static, then calmly said, "CALENDAR."

"You've got ten seconds," Beth said. "Better start spelling."

"CALENDAR is a hard one," Bridget said under her breath. "Real hard."

"C–A–L," Barnaby took a deep breath, "L–A–N–D–E–R."

The wall speaker made a loud, rude honk. Barnaby jumped into the air as if he'd been shocked.

Beth laughed. "It will keep saying the same word until someone gets it right."

"Oh, for Pete's sake," Bridget pushed Barnaby aside. "Let me do it." She stepped onto the black square, and hit the red button with her fist.

"CALENDAR," the speaker said again.

Bridget had a good trick for spelling the word. What makes CALENDAR hard to spell is its middle and its ending. The word sounds as if it ends with LANDER, which is how Barnaby had tried to spell it. But the middle and end of the word should be spelled LENDAR. It is as if a tricky person has switched the E and the A. Bridget remembered that in the middle of CALENDAR is the word LEND. She remembered the phrase, "LEND me a CALENDAR." Confidently, she spelled the word, "C–A–L–E–N–D–A–R!"

The moment Bridget said the final letter, the trapdoor sprang open. The door sprang back, and Bridget was gone.

"Well," Beth said, "who's next?"

"Wow." Barnaby thought it was hard to believe how quickly Bridget had disappeared. It was as if his friend had simply vanished!

"If no one minds," Babette said, "I will go next." The brave French girl stepped onto the black square and pushed the red button.

After another crackle of static, the speaker said the word, "CEMETERY."

Barnaby ran around the room looking at the pages of the dictionary that were pasted up as wallpaper.

"Ten seconds!" Beth yelled.

"C–E–M–E–T–A–R–Y," Babette spelled.

Just as Barnaby found the word, the wall speaker emitted the loud, rude honk.

"Wrong!" Beth said.

As he found the word with his finger—it was near the floor—Barnaby thought it was sort of weird how Beth seemed amused each time any of them made a mistake. After all, they were trying to help *her brother*. How could they save him if they couldn't get out of here?

"It's the end of the word that's hard," he yelled to Babette. "It's E–R–Y, not A–R–Y! There are no *A*s in CEMETERY!"

Beth pushed the red button again.

"CEMETERY," repeated the speaker.

Remembering Barnaby's tip that there are no A's in CEM-ETERY, Babette spelled the word slowly and carefully. "C–E–M–E–T–E–R–Y." The moment she said the final letter, the trapdoor fell open, and Babette vanished.

Beauregard went next. He got the word CONVENIENT and misspelled it CONVENYUNT before Barnaby located it high up on the wall near a picture of Noah Webster. "The last part is I–E–N–T," he yelled.

After the cat spelled CONVENIENT correctly and fell through the trapdoor, Beth said she would go. "Somebody has to look out for your pals." She twirled her braid. "Somebody who knows this palace like the back of her hand." She smiled and slapped the red button.

The speaker said, "HEIGHT."

Without any hesitation, Beth spelled the hard word correctly, "H–E–I–G–H–T."

The trapdoor flipped open, then shut, and Barnaby found himself all alone in the dungeon.

She's a better speller than she said, he thought. The word HEIGHT is hard to spell. It breaks the *I* Before *E* Except After *C* rule. Also, it ends with the weird GHT combination (like TI*GHT*, RI*GHT*, and SI*GHT*).

It was almost as if she knew what she was doing, Barnaby thought. Beth had not seemed even slightly afraid. Her eyes had blazed with excitement. While she spelled the word HEIGHT, she grinned and hunched her shoulders. She looked like a kid about to go on a roller coaster ride. Was it possible that Beth had pushed that button before? Had she fallen through the trapdoor plenty of times? Barnaby was becoming more and more suspicious of Beth, and when he realized this he decided to make the leap and follow his friends.

Barnaby rubbed his bushy red hair. Then he took off his glasses, folded them up, and carefully put them in the pocket of his lab coat where they'd be safe. He walked into the middle of the black square and pushed the button.

The speaker emitted a noise that sounded suspiciously like a chuckle.

"DIFFERENCE," it said.

Barnaby thought for a moment. He closed his eyes and visualized the word, remembering that it had a double F.

He spelled it correctly, "D–I–F–F–E–R–E–N–C–E."

Bang! The trapdoor fell away and Barnaby plummeted through the floor.

Chapter 6:
The Tower

Many spellers have trouble with THEY and the trio of sound-alike words. Do you know what they are and how to spell them?

The moment Barnaby correctly spelled DIFFERENCE, the trapdoor sprang open, and Barnaby dropped through the hole into pitch-black darkness. The trapdoor snapped shut over his head. It was as if he'd fallen into the slippery throat of a long-necked dinosaur! Barnaby slid up, down, and sideways. He felt as if he was traveling at 100 miles per hour. It was as if he were shooting down a water slide. Wham! He hit something, slowed down, spun, and then dropped into something big and soft.

Because he still could not see anything, Barnaby lay on his back for a few seconds and waited for his stomach to catch up with the rest of him. He was so jiggled and joggled that he hardly knew which way was up. Just to be sure he hadn't broken anything important, Barnaby stretched his arms and legs, and wiggled his fingers. "Hey, where am I?"

Barnaby sat up and reached out with one hand. What did he land on? It was a thick blanket. He stood up and groped the blanket with both hands. Nothing seemed to be behind it.

"Hey! Anybody out there?"

No one answered. Barnaby stepped forward. The blanket gave way, and he saw a shaft of light near his toes. He lifted the blanket and found himself in an empty room made of cement blocks—like a room in a warehouse. At one end of the room was a metal door without any windows.

Turning around, Barnaby saw that he had flown out of the mouth of a fat metal pipe and landed on top of an enormous beanbag pillow. If you spelled a word correctly while standing on the trapdoor in the Dungeon, this is the room where you ended up.

"Bridget?" he yelled. "Beauregard? Where are you guys?"

When no one answered, Barnaby crossed the room and went to the door. He placed his ear against it and listened. Did he hear the murmur of voices? "Babette?" Very carefully, he tried the doorknob. It wasn't locked. Slowly, Barnaby turned the knob and opened the door.

On the other side of the door was the foot of a staircase. Barnaby went though the door and looked up the staircase. Although the stairwell was lit up, he couldn't see anything except more steps. He wondered if he was at the very bottom of the Palace of Words, somewhere far below the Dungeon.

Barnaby held his breath and listened. Yeah, he could hear voices all right. He thought of yelling for help, then decided against it. Better to be cautious and not take any chances.

Barnaby tiptoed up the concrete steps. The murmur of voices grew louder. Barnaby climbed up one flight of stairs, then up a second flight.

I know that voice, he thought.

Beth—their new acquaintance, the tall girl with the thick braid—was talking.

"He's noble," Beth said, "that's why. When Biff gives his word, that's it. A herd of crazed elephants couldn't make him change his mind."

"You say the door to his cell in the Tower is unlocked?" Bridget sounded amazed and a little disgusted. "And your brother doesn't even try to escape?"

"He gave the King his word. I wish he'd try to escape. But he's too darn noble ever to go back on his word. Of course, I gotta admit, even if he did, Woof would probably catch him. Woof can smell Biff trying to escape a mile away."

"That horrible animal's not anywhere nearby, is he?" Beauregard sniffed loudly and lashed his tail. "If I see him, I'll scratch his nose!"

Barnaby crept up the steps until he was right behind them. "Boo!"

They all jumped.

"Barnaby!" Bridget cried happily.

"It's about time you showed up," Bridget said. "Now here's the plan. We're going to climb up all these steps," she pointed straight up. Barnaby craned his neck and looked up the stairwell. It seemed to go up and up forever. "And go see Biff, Beth's brother, in his cell in the Tower. Beth says we can walk right in. It's not even locked!"

"Come on!" Beth cried. The tall girl ran ahead of them up the stairs. Her long legs took the steps two or three at a time. Soon, she was out of sight.

"Come on, guys," Bridget said. They started the long climb to the top of the Tower.

By the time the kids got to the top of the last flight of steps, they were covered with sweat. Barnaby felt that his legs would collapse if he had to climb one more step, and his feet felt like they were on fire.

"This must be it," Bridget said. "The door to the Tower. Hey, where's Beth?"

The tall girl was nowhere in sight.

"If you ask me," Barnaby confided in his friends, "there's something funny about that girl. I wonder if she's even got a brother named Biff."

Before anyone could respond, the door flew open. There stood Beth, grinning at them. She looked fresh as a daisy.

"Aren't you exhausted?" Bridget asked. "You must really be in great shape. Did you run up all these flights of steps?" She took off her baseball cap and wiped the sweat off her forehead with the back of her hand. "We're about dead."

Beth grinned crookedly. "How do you spell ELEVATOR?" She winked at them.

Barnaby was so tired from all the climbing that he actually started to spell the word ELEVATOR before he realized it was a joke.

"Ma cherie," Babette said, trying hard to be polite, "do you mean there is an elevator, and you didn't even tell us?" She rubbed the sore muscles in her calves.

"Follow me," Beth said, "he's in his room, er, I mean, in his cell in the Tower. Before we go in, I better warn you." She held her finger to her lips. "Biff's not exactly normal. Not entirely anyway." She tugged her braid.

Bridget said, "Well, how could he be normal, when he's going to be executed at dawn if he doesn't memorize a bunch of words? He's probably crazy with fear. I mean, talk about test anxiety!"

"That's just it. You'd think my brother would be a nervous wreck; you'd think he'd be studying like mad."

"Isn't he?" Babette asked.

"That's why I say he isn't normal. Psychologists call it 'denial.'" Beth folded her long arms and nodded at them as if she really knew what she was talking about.

"Denial? What do you mean?" Barnaby, being more of a chemistry brain, had never really understood the science of psychology.

"Something in my brother's brain turns off, especially when he's under stress. He acts as if nothing's happening. I wouldn't be surprised if he's in there playing with his Gameboy!"

"Gameboy!" Bridget didn't like to say so, but she was nuts about her Gameboy. She loved the thing. As far as she was concerned, any kid who liked his Gameboy couldn't be all that bad.

"Come on." Beth led them to a door and knocked on it.

No one answered.

"Biff? You in there?"

Barnaby was just about to say, 'Ha! I knew it! She doesn't even have a brother,' when Beth eased open the door and stuck in her head. "Hey, Biff!" She pulled back her head and looked at the others. "See what I mean?" She flung open the door.

In the middle of the room, with his back to them, was a good-looking boy with blond hair. He was wearing headphones and dancing like crazy to music they could faintly hear coming from his headphones.

"He should be studying, but look at him. It's sort of sad, really." Beth sighed. "But we gotta be careful. We don't want to startle Biff. Don't mention the execution at dawn, or he'll really go off the deep end." She turned back to her brother. "Biff, honey, you've got visitors!"

Biff must have heard his sister's voice over the din of his music, because he whirled around. He had brilliant blue eyes, and Bridget thought she'd never seen anyone as good looking.

The moment he saw the strangers, Biff whipped off the headphones. "Hey, guys! You friends of my crazy sister?"

Beth stuck her tongue out at him, then made the introductions, telling her brother how the huge dog Woof had captured Barnaby and carried him into the Dungeon. "I got them out through the trapdoor," she explained.

Biff grinned. "That crazy dog!"

Bridget gave him a deeply concerned look. "Are you, um, you know, OK? We heard about the spelling test." Remembering what Beth had just said about how they shouldn't upset Biff, Bridget bit her lip and wished she knew how to keep her mouth shut.

The moment he heard the word *test*, Biff quit grinning. He hung his head. "That darn test. I practically forgot about it. I guess maybe I should be studying."

The kids exchanged looks. Maybe it was true after all. If Biff didn't learn to spell all the words on the list of Fiendishly Hard Words, he'd be executed at dawn.

"Fifty-five words, huh?" Barnaby asked. "That's a lot."

Biff nodded sadly. "I'll never spell them all right. It's hopeless. There are just too many."

"But you can't just give up!" Bridget said.

"You should be studying," Beth said sternly. "Not dancing around like an idiot."

"It's the music," Biff said. "You know, the beat? It just gets into me."

Bridget nodded vigorously. "I'm the same way. When it's a song I like, I just can't stand still!" She was beginning to think that Biff was a pretty good kid. Biff flashed her a broad, friendly smile, and Bridget felt so happy she wanted to hug him. She saw Babette looking at her and smiling.

"We're gonna help him!" Bridget announced. "I don't know how, but we're gonna teach Biff every single one of those fifty-five words!" She gave the others a fierce look as if they'd better not give her any argument, or they'd regret it.

Biff sighed. Bridget thought he was the cutest boy she'd ever seen in her life. He was so darn cute, it hurt her heart just to look at him.

"I guess you're right. I should be studying," Biff said. Then he looked up and winked at them. It made Bridget laugh out loud. She thought he was such a brave guy. Here he is, right on the verge of getting executed by the cruel King of the Palace, and he's laughing about it! Maybe he doesn't even need to study. Maybe he really is a great speller.

"How about this?" Barnaby said. "We give Biff a practice test. Then we'll know how many words he needs to work on."

"Barnaby, that is a fabulous idea," Babette said.

Beth yawned. She sat down in a chair and picked up a magazine.

Looking around the room for writing supplies, Barnaby thought the cell at the top of the Tower looked a lot like a typical kid's bedroom. Three Michael Jordan posters were taped to one wall; a pile of games was stacked in one corner; and the bookshelf was full of science fiction and *Goosebumps* magazines.

"Here's some paper and a pencil," Bridget yelled.

Biff looked sadly at his headphones as if he'd really like to listen to music and dance some more, but then he put them down and took the pad of paper and the pencil from Bridget. "OK, give it to me. Let's get it over with." He pointed to a piece of paper thumbtacked to a wall. "That's the list."

On the wall was the same list of Fiendishly Hard Words, the list of words most frequently misspelled by junior high kids that they had seen down in the Dungeon.

Biff sat cross-legged on his bed with a pad of paper in his lap.

Babette read out the words one at a time and Biff wrote them on the pad of paper, concentrating on spelling them correctly. When he was all done, he handed the pad of paper to Bridget.

"How'd I do?" he asked hopefully.

Bridget scanned the list. Her heart fell. "Not so good." She looked up at the others. "In fact—terrible." She looked sympathetically at Biff. "Sorry to be so blunt, but I have to tell it like it is."

"Did he get *any* right?" Babette asked.

"A few." Bridget handed the list to Barnaby.

"Wow," Barnaby said, looking at all the mistakes, "it's going to be a long night."

Babette was looking thoughtfully at the list of words. "I've got an idea," she said. "We will divide up this list. It's too long for anyone to learn all at once."

"What a great idea!" Bridget snatched the list out of Babette's hand. "Where should we start? Let's see." She pointed at several words on the list. "Look at this, there are a lot of contractions. And lots of 'there' words."

"Then that's it!" Barnaby declared. "That's how we'll start." He gave Biff a reassuring pat on his shoulder and announced with confidence, "One way or another, we're going to teach you how to spell all these words. Tomorrow morning when you take that test, you'll get a perfect score!"

Aa Bb Cc Dd Ee Ff Gg Hh Ii Jj

Exercises for Chapter 6

Exercise 1: They, There, Their, and They're

Like Biff, a lot of spellers have trouble with the word THEY and the trio of sound-alike words, THERE, THEIR, and THEY'RE. It is extremely easy to get them confused. If you work on getting them right, you can eliminate a lot of the most common errors!

THEY is a little hard to spell because it sounds as if it contains an A. Remember this: "THEY starts with THE."

THEIR means "belonging to them." THEIR yo-yo; THEIR squirt gun; THEIR Gameboy. Notice that THEIR is one of those "rule-breaking" words. It contains the I and E pair, but in this case, just to make you a little crazy, the I comes *after* the E. One way to remember how to spell this tricky word is to remember that same little saying, "THEIR starts with THE."

THEY'RE is a contraction of THEY ARE. "THEY'RE pretty nasty monsters, but fortunately they only eat grown-ups."

THERE is a direction and the opposite of HERE, (which is a word embedded in T*HERE*). Remember that HERE is part of THERE and it will help you remember how to spell this word. "All of the vampires in this town live over THERE." We also use phrases like "THERE is" and "THERE are." "THERE ARE way too many werewolves living in this town!"

These three words (THEIR, THEY'RE, and THERE) are not really all that hard to spell, but it is easy to get them confused. Also, since they are all real words, if you make a mistake and use the wrong form of the word, the spell checker on your computer will never catch it! When you are proofreading your writing and you see one of these words, it will help to ask yourself, "Did I use the right spelling? In this case, does the word mean which of the following: belonging to (THEIR), a contraction standing for they are (THEY'RE), or direction or basically any other usage of the word (THERE)?"

Try doing these examples. Some of them are a little goofy, but that just makes them more fun. Each sentence contains one of the three sound-alike words, THERE, THEIR, or THEY'RE. Write the correct form of the word in each blank space. Check your work by looking at the answers in the back of the book.

1. If they bring _____ tarantula over here one more time, I'm going to stomp on it!

2. I'm just guessing, but I think the Invisible Man is sitting right over_____ .

3. Where does the most verbose teacher in the world live? Right over _____ .

4. _____ restaurant has pretty good food, but watch out for the cockroaches!

5. All the space aliens say _____ going to hang out at the new mall.

6. _____ are three ghouls living under that bridge.

7. _____ football team has the cutest quarterback I've ever seen.

8. When we opened the coffin, no one was in _____ !

9. If you ask me, _____ just a bunch of gorillas.

10. _____ is only one way that monster can get through that locked door.

see page 249 for answers

Exercise 2: Tricky Contractions

Several of the most common spelling errors are words with apostrophes. If you can get the hang of these words, you can get rid of a lot of mistakes! Notice that in several of these words, the apostrophe does *not* mean the possessive (a possessive means belonging to, as in: *Rachel's* eye is red because she scratched it). Apostrophe words that are not possessives are just cases in which two words are slurred together and a letter is missing from the second word. That's why these words are tricky!

DOESN'T—means DOES NOT. Again, notice that the apostrophe signals a missing letter. The O in NOT is missing.

DON'T—means DO NOT. This word seems easy, but some kids put the apostrophe in the wrong place. DO'NT is a mistake. Try this trick to remember how to spell it: the apostrophe signals that the O in NOT is missing.

IT'S—one of the easiest words to mess up. IT'S means IT IS. The I is missing from IS. The possessive form of IT does NOT have the apostrophe—its doghouse, its tank.

LET'S—means LET US. The apostrophe signals that the U is missing from US.

THAT'S—means THAT IS. The I is missing from IS.

THERE'S—means THERE IS. The I is missing from IS. Notice that when you use the *possessive* THEIRS, you leave out the apostrophe.

YOU'RE—means YOU ARE. The apostrophe signals that the A in ARE is missing. The common mistake is to write YOUR when you should write YOU'RE.

Exercise 3: Using the Tricky Contractions

Put the apostrophe where it belongs in each of the following sentences.

1. <u>Thats</u> as far as we go.

2. <u>Its</u> about time you showed up.

3. <u>Dont</u> go into that cave!

4. It <u>doesnt</u> matter if you do have three heads. I love you—all three of you! Well, two of you anyway!

5. <u>Youre</u> kind of cute—for a chinless lizard.

6. <u>Lets</u> jump into the swimming pool—never mind my pet shark.

7. <u>Theres</u> one million dollars in this suitcase. I wonder who it belongs to.

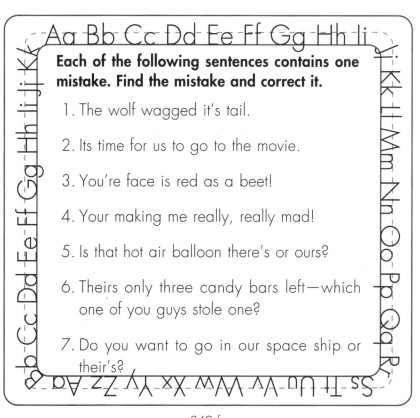

Each of the following sentences contains one mistake. Find the mistake and correct it.

1. The wolf wagged it's tail.

2. Its time for us to go to the movie.

3. You're face is red as a beet!

4. Your making me really, really mad!

5. Is that hot air balloon there's or ours?

6. Theirs only three candy bars left—which one of you guys stole one?

7. Do you want to go in our space ship or their's?

see page 249 for answers

Chapter 7:
The Truth Comes Out

MOTIVATION!
It's the key
to learning
how to spell
(or do anything
else) well!

Biff soon got the hang of the THERE-THEIR-THEY'RE words. When he applied himself, he learned rapidly. Encouraged by Bridget and Barnaby, he quickly mastered the Tricky Contractions. Once he realized that what makes those particular contractions so easy to misspell is the fact that their apostrophes don't signal possession, but reveal that a letter is missing, he caught on fast. When he'd finally learned them, he flopped backwards and sprawled full length on the floor as if he had completely exhausted himself.

Barnaby laughed.

"Need a break, huh?" Bridget said. By then she was hopelessly in love with Biff and had begun to pity herself. Although she fell in love with boys on a regular basis, they never seemed to fall in love with her.

Biff sat up and held his knees. He fixed his blue eyes on Bridget. "You guys are great, you and Barnaby. Really! But…well, may I ask a question? If you don't mind."

"Sure!" Bridget hoped like crazy that Biff was going to ask her to go to a dance or to a movie or—best of all—a baseball game.

"How come you guys are helping me so much?"

Bridget blinked at him in amazement. "The test," she said at last. She'd forgotten it for a moment herself. Biff was in great danger. Tomorrow morning, if he didn't pass the test and get a perfect score, he definitely wasn't going to ask her or anyone else to a baseball game. "The cruel King. You know." She was afraid to say it out loud.

Barnaby sat down beside them. "Don't worry, Biff. We're definitely not going to let it happen. We're going to save you!"

Biff cocked his head to one side and looked at Barnaby for a full ten seconds. "From what?"

"From what?!" Bridget slapped her knee. "From execution!"

Biff stared at her. Then he stared at Barnaby. Finally, he stood up. "Beth! I mean it, you come here this minute!"

Beth was trying to sneak quietly out the door.

"You tell them, Beth!" Biff yelled. "I'm not kidding. You tell them this very minute!"

Beth stopped; she had her hand on the doorknob.

"If you don't tell them, I will," Biff said sternly.

Beth came slowly into the middle of the room. She grinned crookedly. "Do you know what I told you—about how if Biff doesn't learn all the fifty-five words, he'll be executed?"

"At dawn, you said," Bridget reminded her.

"That wasn't entirely true."

Biff stared at his sister with his mouth open. "What else did you tell them?"

"Well, there was the part about how the King and Queen are cruel monsters." Beth twisted her braid. "That wasn't exactly true either."

"You said the King threw a dictionary at Biff and told him to memorize it," Barnaby said. "You said the King and Queen were the meanest people on Earth!"

Barnaby, Bridget, Babette, and Beauregard circled around the tall girl and glared at her.

"You told them that?" Biff said in disbelief. "You said he threw a dictionary at me? The nice old King?"

"As you know," Beth smiled sweetly, "I am an uncontrollable liar. I couldn't help myself."

"The King and Queen," Biff said loudly, "are the kindest, sweetest, most generous people in the world. They are wonderful! You told these kids they're cruel?"

"You met them," Beth told the other kids, "when you were out there on the sidewalk behind the Palace." She pointed a long, slender arm toward a window. "I was standing right up here watching. The King and Queen were on their way to an elementary school. They like to read stories to little kids."

"That nice old couple," Barnaby said.

"The tall old lady," Beauregard remembered.

"The plump old gentleman," recalled Babette.

Bridget stuck a piece of bubble gum in her mouth and chewed rapidly. Barnaby stuck both hands into his bushy red hair and rubbed it every which way. Beauregard lashed his tail, and Babette lifted her sunglasses to get a better look at the tall girl who had told them so many amazing whoppers.

"It was just a joke," Beth said. She looked a little nervous. "Don't you guys have any sense of humor?"

Bridget said, "You told us Biff was going to be killed!"

It took awhile for all the truth to come out. It turned out that Beth had been looking out the window earlier and had seen the kids talking to the Guard of Spelling. She'd opened the window and heard the Guard give them difficult words to spell. She'd seen the Guard allow Beauregard to enter the Palace, then slam the door in the faces of Barnaby, Bridget, and Babette. It was Beth who had written the word RHYTHM on a piece of paper, then used it to wrap up a key. She'd tossed it down to them.

"It was your arm we saw!" Bridget stomped her foot. "I oughta give you a good sock in the nose."

The giant dog Woof had grabbed Barnaby because Beth had let the dog loose and told him to capture the first person he saw and carry him down to the Dungeon.

"Woof used to save stranded mountain climbers," Biff explained. "We can't break him of the habit. If you tell him to, he'll carry anybody anywhere."

Barnaby had to admit that although the dog had carried him all the way to the Dungeon, Woof had handled him gently, carrying him by the seat of his pants. "When Woof set me down, he actually licked me. At the time, I thought he was going to eat me, but maybe…"

"He's just friendly," Biff explained. He told them that the Dungeon was not a real dungeon but a classroom. "It's a fun place to learn things!" The trapdoor, he explained, was a fun slide designed to encourage kids to learn to spell difficult words. "Didn't you think it was cool going down the slide? The King and Queen want learning to be fun. That's the whole idea of the Palace!"

Barnaby had to admit that running around the room looking up words on the dictionary pages pasted to the walls of the Dungeon had certainly taught him how to spell the difficult words. Whizzing down the dark slide had been scary but very exciting.

Bridget stomped her foot. "I don't care. She told us some whopping lies, and I'm mad!"

Someone laughed. Someone threw back her head and laughed loudly.

"Babette?" Bridget said. "Are you okay?"

"Motivation," the French girl said.

"What?"

"My mother is a teacher back in France," Babette explained. "She always says that the hardest thing in teaching is motivation. A motivated kid is easy to teach. An unmotivated student is practically impossible to teach." She smiled at Beth. "Today, we've all had a great lesson in motivation."

"What do you mean?" Barnaby asked.

"Well, look at all we've learned. I've mastered several new words. And what about you, Beauregard? Tell us the truth, haven't you learned how to spell several difficult words?"

Beauregard wiggled his whiskers thoughtfully, then admitted that he had learned lots of new words. He listed several of them, "STOMACHACHE, GYPSY, RHYTHM, ASSISTANT." He paused and yelled, "'There's an ANT in ASSISTANT!' I learned some useful spelling rules from the Duchess like 'I Before E Except After C.' And then, in the elevator, I learned that the rules don't always work. I learned to spell FRIEND and BELIEVE and WEIRD. In the Dungeon, I learned to spell CONVENIENT. It sounds as if it is spelled with Y–U–N–T, but really it ends with I–E–N–T. That's how I got the trapdoor to fall open. Come to think of it, you know what?" He lashed his tail excitedly. "Helping Biff, I've learned even more words. I've learned the THERE–THEIR–THEY'RE words. It's easy to learn new words when you've got other people helping you and encouraging you. I even learned the Tricky Contractions!"

Babette smiled, "You see what I mean? We've all learned new words. And why? Motivation! Because each time it was a challenge or a game."

Biff interrupted, "You know what? I put off learning that list of Fiendishly Hard Words. Usually, I hate studying. I especially hate studying spelling! I've had that list of words for a week, but not until you guys showed up and encouraged me did I study it. It was actually fun!" Biff told them that if he mastered all the words on the list by tomorrow, he'd get a prize. "The King and Queen will take me to a baseball game." He grinned. "It's no secret, but I'm a total nut about the Yankees. If I get all fifty-five words right, I even get to take a friend."

"You see, kids," Babette said, "strange as it seems, we ought to thank Beth. She is indeed an uncontrollable liar, but she is also an excellent teacher. Because of her, we've each learned how to spell many new words. I even think that, with a little more help, Biff may get to go to that ball game after all."

Bridget cleared her throat.

The others all looked at Bridget. Would she blow her stack? She absolutely hated being lied to.

Bridget adjusted her baseball cap so that its bill pointed sideways. She balled up her fists and looked straight at Beth.

The tall girl took a step backward; she raised her hands fearfully.

Bridget folded her arms and blew a bubble. She made the bubble bigger and bigger until it popped. "Aw, I hate to hold a grudge," she said. "Hey, Biff, do you really want to go to that ball game?"

"Yes!" Biff said.

"Then I forgive you, Tall Stuff," Bridget said. She shook hands with Beth.

The tall girl looked extremely relieved she'd gotten off so easily.

Bridget turned around, grinned at all her friends, and clapped her hands. "Come on, if we're gonna help Biff win those tickets, we've got a lot more work to do!"

Exercises for Chapter 7

To help Biff win the trip to the ballpark, Bridget and Barnaby helped him with several more of the words on the list of Fiendishly Hard Words.

The "Every" Words and Other Compound Words

If you can master the words below, you will have conquered a big part of the list. Learn the words below and then do the exercise that follows to make sure that what you've read has stuck in your brain.

The word EVERY is a little tricky to spell. When pronounced, it sounds as if it has only two syllables, so it is easy to suppose that it is spelled EVRY. The trick to spelling it correctly is remembering the E in the middle of EVERY.

Compound words are two other words that are joined together. They are not all that hard to spell, but it is easy to forget that they are really one word, not two. Four EVERY words are on the list of Fiendishly Hard Words:

EVERYBODY
EVERYONE
EVERYTHING
EVERYWHERE

Here are several more compound words. It is easy to forget that each of them is supposed to be one word, not two.

ALWAYS (do not spell it "all ways")

ANYTHING

MAYBE

SOMEONE

SOMETIME

SOMETHING

There is one commonly misspelled word that people tend to think should be a compound word, but it really isn't. That word is: A LOT.

A LOT (two words, not one. This word is not a compound and should *not* be spelled ALOT)

Three holidays and one of the days of the week are also on the list.

CHRISTMAS (people tend to forget the T. It helps to remember that Christmas is the birthday of Jesus CHRIST)

EASTER (don't forget the A; there is an EAST in EASTER)

HALLOWEEN (remember that there is a double L and a double E)

SATURDAY (not SATERDAY)

Each of the following sentences contains one mistake. Find the mistake and correct it.

1. Next Eester, we are all going to visit your aunt.

2. Every body jump into the pool!

3. Listen! Some one is in our attic!

4. We all ways love to go shark fishing.

5. May be I will go or may be I won't.

6. My favorite holiday is Chrissmas.

7. Yeah, well, my favorite holiday is Haloween.

8. Next Saterday is the big football game.

9. I want every one in this room to raise their hand.

10. I know I've forgotten some thing; I just can't remember what.

11. Every thing in this box is extremely valu-able, so don't lose it.

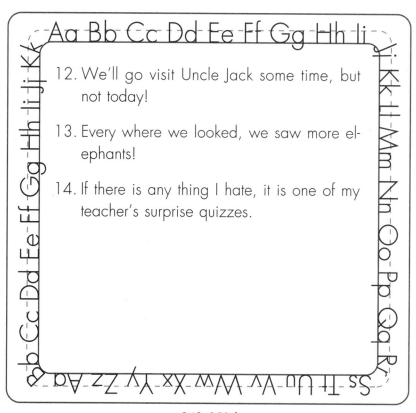

12. We'll go visit Uncle Jack some time, but not today!

13. Every where we looked, we saw more elephants!

14. If there is any thing I hate, it is one of my teacher's surprise quizzes.

see pages 249–250 for answers

You can make up a trick to learn how to spell every word. The trick to spelling EVERY is to say: "There is an E in the middle of EVERY.

Chapter 8:
The King and Queen Return

Do you know the difference between the words ACCEPT and EXCEPT? They are actually opposite in meaning.

Biff worked hard until he mastered all the words on the list of Fiendishly Hard Words and the words in the exercises at the end of the last chapter. While Bridget quizzed him on how to spell the words, Biff wandered around his room (it was not really a cell but a bedroom), yelling out the letters.

When he had finally learned all of the new words, he said, "I definitely need a break. If I study any more, my head is going to blow up!"

"What you need," Bridget suggested, "is some exercise."

"Hey, Babette," said Barnaby. "How about giving us some lessons?" He leapt to his feet, stuck out his hands, and yelled, "Hi-yah!"

Babette smiled and gracefully leapt to her feet. "It would be a pleasure." She bowed.

One of the many remarkable things about Babette was that she was an expert at karate. Pretty soon, the three of them were leaping, spinning, and kicking all over the bedroom.

While her friends were occupied, Bridget sat on the bed. She would have talked to Beth except that, soon after the spelling lesson began, Beth yawned and said she was bored to death. She was going to her room to read a book. Bridget examined the list, deciding what words Biff should work on next.

Beauregard pressed himself into a corner to avoid the flying hands and feet. He wiggled his whiskers and wondered if the kids were going to get into any more trouble today. He lashed his tail, sniffed the air, and wondered if that awful dog Woof could be anywhere nearby.

"Hey, what's that?" asked Bridget. She looked up from the list.

The others came to a stop. "What is it?" asked Babette. Her cheeks were slightly flushed and she was panting a little.

There was a gentle tapping at the door.

"Who is it?" Biff ran to the door and threw it open. "Hey, look who's here! Come in, come in!"

Biff led a tall, skinny woman and a short, plump man into his bedroom.

"It is the King and the Queen," Babette said. "How nice to meet your majesties." She curtseyed.

Bridget watched the French girl in amazement; she had never curtseyed in her life, and she wasn't sure she even knew how to do it.

Barnaby bowed, and Beauregard flourished his tail over his head and purred.

"Oh, you don't need to call us that," said the King.

"We aren't real royalty, you know," the Queen explained.

"We are fake from our heads to our toes." The King smiled and nodded his head.

"Call me Mom," said the nice old lady.

"Call me Pop," said the kindly old gentleman.

Biff explained that the kids and Beauregard had been teaching him to spell the words on the list of Fiendishly Hard Words. "I've learned lots of them already. These kids are great teachers!"

"Mom," said Pop, "I told you they were remarkable. Didn't I tell you so?"

"You certainly did, Pop. When we first met them, that is exactly what you said."

"And they've been teaching Biff the list of words. Why, I think we may have to take all of them to a ball game before this is over."

The King explained that he and the Queen had been trying to help Biff with his spelling all week without much success. "Biff is very good at math. He loves sports, but it is hard to get him to work on his spelling." Pop smiled tolerantly at Biff. "We thought maybe the reward of the baseball game would be a good incentive."

"We should have thought of it before," said the Queen. "What Biff obviously needed was other kids to be his study partners. He's such a sociable boy. His sister Beth loves to learn by herself, but Biff requires company."

The Queen explained that just as kids come in all shapes and sizes, they have all sorts of ways of learning new things. "If one method doesn't work, try another!"

To Barnaby, Bridget, and Babette, this certainly seemed like sensible advice.

Biff said, "Mom and Pop, why not tell these guys how you got this Palace?" He looked at the others. "It's a great story."

"We got this Palace from Chick," the Queen said.

"The Chicken King," the King added. "Have you heard of him?" Chick the Chicken King was famous; the commercials for his fried chicken restaurants were on TV night and day. The Chicken King often appeared in these commercials. He was fond of wearing a chicken suit complete with bright yellow feathers and a vivid red rooster's comb. Everyone who watched TV knew who he was.

"We were junior high school teachers, you see," the Queen said, "oh, for years and years."

"Chick was our former student."

"He was a perfectly awful speller, but an A+ at arithmetic."

"And very fond of chicken!" the King added.

"Biff reminds me of him a little, don't you think, Pop?"

"Chick went into business—the chicken restaurant business. Oh, and my, he was very successful."

"Stunningly successful!" the Queen said. "Soon, Chick was swimming in money. He had chicken restaurants everywhere. So many that I don't know how he ever keeps track of them all. He built this Palace—the Chicken King's Palace!"

The King held his hands together and hung his head sadly. "But one day, something quite awful happened."

"Something most tragic," agreed the Queen.

"Chick's beloved brother, Bill, and Bill's lovely wife, Anne, both died, abruptly." The King wiped away a tear.

"A mountain-climbing accident." The Queen took her husband's arm and gave it a comforting squeeze.

"Leaving behind two small children."

Biff grinned. "This is where we come in."

The King and Queen looked fondly at Biff.

"You don't mean it!" Bridget said.

Babette said, "Excuse me, have I missed something important?"

Barnaby yelled, "Don't you get it? Biff and Beth are the kids of the Chicken King!"

"Not his kids," the King said, "they are the kids of his brother Bill. Biff and Beth are the nephew and niece of the Chicken King. After the death of Bill and his lovely wife, Anne, Beth and Biff became his wards. Chick was their godfather, you see."

"I was two," Biff said, "and Beth was three. We don't really remember our parents very well. Beth remembers them a little. She remembers our mother's smiles and our father's deep voice. All I remember is that my mother would hold me in her lap and she smelled of perfume. Like lilacs."

Bridget thought this was the saddest story she'd ever heard. Biff was an orphan! On the other hand, if you had to be brought up by someone besides your parents, well, you could not do any better than this nice old couple.

"The Chicken King is your uncle?" Barnaby was practically addicted to the Chicken King's fried chicken, especially the barbecue variety. There was a Chicken King only two blocks from his house, and he was forever begging his parents to order boxes of their delicious chicken.

"After the disaster, Chick came to us," the King said.

"The dear man felt he needed help," the Queen explained. "He was so busy, you see. And unmarried—a confirmed bachelor, I'm afraid, with no experience raising children."

"He asked us to raise Beth and Biff. We'd just retired from teaching and really did need something to keep us busy."

"He knew they'd be great parents! And they have been too!" Biff ran to the Queen and gave her a big hug, which she gladly returned.

"Biff's Uncle Chick gave us this huge Palace," the King explained. "And a ridiculously large sum of money, too. The man is generous to a fault. He still visits often because he loves to see his niece and nephew but is happy with his decision to have us raise them."

"Ever since," Biff yelled, "they've been giving the money away. They've turned this place into a sort of school, a free school where kids can learn all sorts of things in a fun way, where no one takes attendance, and there are never any grades!"

"We love to teach, especially reading and writing," the Queen said. "And spelling, of course. We think nothing is more useful to people than good writing skills. Isn't that right, dear? Don't you think teaching keeps us young?"

Beauregard stepped forward; he stood up on his hind legs and waved his tail grandly. "About spelling, don't you agree with the Duchess of Rules, that English spelling would be much improved if it was made orderly, if it was—well, you know—simplified?"

"No disrespect to the Duchess," the King said. He cleared his throat. "But I beg to differ. English is called English—and of course it comes, mostly, from the country England. But it left there long ago and traveled all over the world. For centuries, English has been growing and growing. It's immensely popular you know, even in countries such as India. English is even widely spoken in Africa. There is no one person or even one country in charge. English belongs as much to Canada and Australia, to India and the United States as it does to England.

English belongs to all the hundreds of millions of people who speak it and read it and spell it! It is a world language. Of course, certain words are terribly tricky to spell. As a result, everyone makes mistakes. Even the best writers make a few spelling mistakes! Did you know that? Mom and I think that it is important to preserve the spelling just the way it is now— it is a kind of honor, a tribute to the places and times where all those words came from. Besides, it can be fun to work on spelling. That's what we think anyway, don't we, Mom?"

Mom said, "Of course I agree, Pop. But you do go on. That was quite a speech!"

The King blushed.

"While we've got you answering questions," Barnaby said, "I'd like to ask one."

"By all means, dear," the Queen said, "what's bothering you?"

"What I don't understand is, well, if this place is supposed to be fun, well, I hate to say it but…"

"Go ahead, don't be afraid to say what's on your mind," the King said.

"What about this Guard of Spelling? He just about scared us to death. He threatened to cut off our heads!"

"Oh, dear," the Queen said. She looked at the King. "You'll have to talk to him again, dear."

"I hope you noticed that his sword doesn't have a blade," the King said gently.

"We had to take away the blade," the Queen said, "we were afraid he might hurt himself."

"He's rude!" Bridget said. "I think he should be fired! He's tricky too. I think he actually likes it when kids make mistakes."

"He tossed me in the Dungeon!" Beauregard said. "Just because I misspelled the word WEIRD!"

"Well, that's what I wanted to ask," Barnaby said. "How come you don't get rid of him? The Guard of Spelling's no fun at all!"

The Queen sighed. "It's a long story."

"Go on, Mom," Biff said, "tell them all about it. It's an interesting story."

"It is a sad story," the Queen said. "Let me see, where to begin? Well, you should know that the Guard of Spelling is my brother Pete."

"Your brother!" exclaimed Bridget.

"And the Duchess of Rules is the King's sister. She never married, you see, and neither did the Guard. When we moved here to the Palace, we invited them to live with us. It was Chick's idea for us to dress up like royalty, to entertain the kids, you know. I was the Queen, and Pop here was the King! It was a silly idea, but at first we thought there was no harm in it. It's great fun to be Queen, even if only for pretend. I had the loveliest crown. You should have seen it. And of course, if Pop and I were royalty, we had to let Pete be at least a lord. He designed the Guard's uniform himself. Oh, he was terribly proud of it! And we made Ruthie, Pop's sister, into a Duchess. And then, we all lived quite happily together. We raised Beth and Biff and we started our school. You should see our library—a lovely collection of books. And then, the most wonderful thing happened."

Biff interrupted enthusiastically, "Ruthie and Pete fell in love!"

"In love?" Bridget could hardly believe anyone could possibly fall in love with the stiff old Guard of Spelling! But Beauregard remembered the compliments the Duchess had paid the Guard after he had left them alone in the sewing room. It seemed to the cat that the Duchess was still in love with the Guard.

"What happened?" asked Babette. "Did something happen?"

"One day, Pete decided to propose to Ruthie. He came to Pop here and told him his plans. And Pop and I at once started to plan a wedding. Can you imagine? We could have a wonderful wedding here in the Palace, with lots of kids in attendance! Pete went to see Ruthie. We knew we were being very naughty, but Pop and I stood outside the door and tried to listen. We could hear almost nothing, only the murmur of Pete's voice. He has such a fine, low voice."

"And then we heard a THUMP!" the King cried.

"A terribly loud thump!" agreed the Queen. "And Ruthie began to scream! We opened the door and ran into the room."

"And there was Pete," the King said. "Out like a light, with Ruthie leaning over him and sobbing her eyes out."

"But what happened?" Barnaby asked. "What knocked him out?"

"We don't know," the Queen said. "We fear we never will know. Ruthie says he just collapsed."

The King nodded sadly, "When it comes to that question, we've resigned ourselves to living in darkness. I went and got a glass of water and dumped it on poor old Pete's face."

"He came to? He woke up?" Beauregard asked.

"He awoke and saw his uniform," the Queen said, "and ever since he's been the Guard of Spelling in earnest. He believes Pop and I are a real King and a genuine Queen, and Ruthie a real Duchess."

"Since he got knocked out, he thinks it is his job to guard spelling," the King said. "Old Pete's meek as a lamb really, and wouldn't hurt a fly, but you'd never know it. He thinks that he has to act ferociously and wear that suit of armor. We humor him, you see."

"But can't you set him straight?" Barnaby asked. "Can't you just tell him it's all just play-acting?"

"We've tried, Barnaby, many times," the Queen said. "Haven't we, Pop?"

"Pete grows terribly disturbed, son," the King explained. "It's a miserable thing to see. He gets red in the face; his eyes grow confused. He commences to weep, and then he falls into a dead faint."

"And when he awakes," said the Queen, "he's back to thinking he's the Guard of Spelling again."

"And what about Ruthie," Babette asked, "what about the Duchess?"

"She's had the worst misfortune of all," said the King. "Pete's forgotten what he was doing that day. He has forgotten he was proposing, forgotten he was ever in love."

"Ruthie is heartbroken," the Queen agreed. "She thinks Pete will never get back to his old self. So long as Ruthie pretends she is a real Duchess and that he is a real Guard, Pete likes to visit with her, but he never remembers he was once going to ask her to marry him. She continues to hope, of course. I guess people can always hope."

"Like she said," the King said, "it's a sad story. But I guess you see why we don't fire him. Under the circumstances."

The kids all agreed that, considering everything, it would be wrong to fire the Guard of Spelling.

"Well, I think we need a treat to cheer everyone up!" the Queen cried. "I've never seen so many serious faces! Come on, Pop, let's go get some ice cream."

"Excellent idea," said the King. He held the door for open her Majesty.

"Biff, dear, why don't you work on the rest of that list?" the Queen said as she and the King went out the door. "And maybe tomorrow, we will take everyone to a ball game!"

Exercises for Chapter 8

Bridget picked out the following commonly mis-spelled words for Biff to work on.

BUY—easy to confuse with BY. BUY means *purchase*; it contains a silent U. "I've decided to BUY this skateboard." The other spelling has many meanings, including *near to* or *along*: "Doesn't he live BY the river?"

EXCEPT—easy to confuse with the word AC-CEPT. EXCEPT means *with the exclusion of*, or *but*. "You can all go EXCEPT Bob." It also means, were it not for the fact that, only. "I would go with you to the dance except I already said I would go with Jack." When used as a verb, EXCEPT means *to leave out*, or *exclude*. ACCEPT means *to receive gladly*, or *to answer affirmatively*. "I will ACCEPT that package." "When he asked if I would take the job, I said, 'I ACCEPT.'"

FINALLY—like PROBABLY, it is easy to forget that middle syllable, and misspell it "FINLY" or "FINELY." Don't forget this word has three syl-lables: FIN–AL–LY. Some people like to remem-ber that FINALLY starts with the word FINAL, with an LY tacked onto the end.

NO—this little word is easy to spell, but some people get it confused with the sound-alike word KNOW. NO is the opposite of YES. To KNOW is *to understand* or *recognize*. "NO, I won't go!" "I KNOW the answer to that question."

OUR—easy to confuse with HOUR, as in time. "OUR house," but "It takes one HOUR to walk there."

PROBABLY—when said quickly, this word sounds as if it might be spelled "PROBLY" or "PROBBLY." Don't forget the middle syllable: PROB–AB–LY.

THROUGH—this word is often misspelled THRU. It is easy to confuse with the word THOR-OUGH, which means *complete*. "We went THROUGH the tunnel." "His report was very de-tailed and THOROUGH." Remember that THROUGH ends with the word ROUGH. Some kids like to remember the saying: THROUGH is ROUGH to spell!

TOO—this commonly misspelled word is easy to confuse with the sound-alike words TO and TWO. TOO means *also*, or *as well*. "Can I go, TOO?" It also means excessively: TOO much, TOO hot. The number is spelled TWO. TO is a little word with several meanings: *In a direction toward* or *in the direction of*; *In contact with*, or

Aa Bb Cc Dd Ee Ff Gg Hh Ii Jj

cheek TO cheek; *Through and including*: from four TO six o'clock; *For* or *of*: that belt belongs TO this dress. TO is also the first part of infinitive verbs: TO run, TO jump, TO fall.

WENT—this word seems easy to spell, but some people think it must be like WHICH and WHERE and spell it WHENT. This word is actually an easy one because WENT is spelled exactly as it sounds.

WHERE—people tend to think it must have an A in it and misspell it WEAR, WARE, or WERE. All three of these are real words, so a computer spellchecker won't catch these mistakes. Remember that WHERE starts with WH and does not contain an A. Think of this: "You are HERE, so *WHERE* are you going?"

WHICH—people tend to misspell it WITCH. A WITCH is a legendary old lady who rides around on a broom and hangs out with black cats. Remember that WHICH starts with WH and does not have a T. "Which way are you going?" "The WITCH cast a spell on Mary."

Find and correct the mistakes in the following sentences. Notice that some sentences have more than one error. The number of spelling mistakes is noted in parentheses at the end of the sentences.

1. The which rubbed the wart on the end of her nose and wondered where she could get a bat's tongue. (1)

2. We whent down the river by canoe. (1)

3. Witch way are you going? (1)

4. Twenty bucks for a baseball card? That's way to much! (1)

5. One or too of you girls stand over there beside the wall. (1)

6. I want too by a half dozen peaches. (2)

7. In one our it will be midnight. (1)

8. Do you want to come over to hour house? (1)

9. The best way to get there is to cut thru the park. (1)

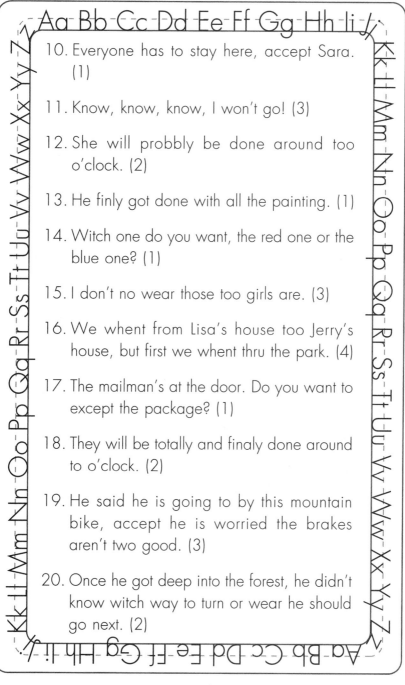

Aa Bb Cc Dd Ee Ff Gg Hh Ii Jj

10. Everyone has to stay here, accept Sara. (1)

11. Know, know, know, I won't go! (3)

12. She will probbly be done around too o'clock. (2)

13. He finly got done with all the painting. (1)

14. Witch one do you want, the red one or the blue one? (1)

15. I don't no wear those too girls are. (3)

16. We whent from Lisa's house too Jerry's house, but first we whent thru the park. (4)

17. The mailman's at the door. Do you want to except the package? (1)

18. They will be totally and finaly done around to o'clock. (2)

19. He said he is going to by this mountain bike, accept he is worried the brakes aren't two good. (3)

20. Once he got deep into the forest, he didn't know witch way to turn or wear he should go next. (2)

see page 250 for answers

When used as a verb, EXCEPT means *to leave out*, or *to exclude*. ACCEPT means *to receive gladly, to answer affirmatively.*

Chapter 9:
Beth's Secret

If a talking
cat can learn
to spell, so
can you!

The King and Queen returned with big aluminum bowls full of vanilla ice cream for all of them. Bridget licked the last drops from her spoon. "Biff has learned almost all of the Fiendishly Hard Words," she told their Majesties. "I counted. There are only twelve left."

Biff grinned with pleasure. "I've never learned so many words all at once in my life." He confessed to Bridget, "Beth is great at spelling, but I really stink. Usually, I mean. Except when you're helping me. You're really a great teacher! Beauregard's learning a lot, too!"

Bridget smiled with delight. She loved to be complimented.

The Queen patted Biff on the shoulder and told him she thought that perhaps he'd had enough studying for the day. "You've done a wonderful job, Biff. Why not learn the rest tomorrow morning?"

"Nope," Biff pushed back his hair, "I'm learning the last dozen. I'm on a roll, and I don't want to cool off until I'm done. Besides, Bridget, didn't you say some of them are easy?"

Bridget peered hard at the list, "OFF," she said. "I mean, how easy is that? OFF?" She laughed. "How could anyone misspell OFF?"

Biff nodded. "O–F," he said confidently.

Beth's face fell. "What'd you say?"

"O–F," Biff repeated loudly, "that spells OFF."

Beauregard rose up on his hind legs. "I beg to differ, young man." He flourished his tail. "The word OFF is spelled," he tapped the side of his furry head with his paw, "A–W–F."

Bridget sighed. "I guess OFF isn't as easy to spell as I thought. Come on, Biff, it looks as if we've got a lot more work to do."

The King and Queen began collecting the empty ice cream bowls.

"Barnaby," Bridget said, "you work with Beauregard. I'll work with Biff. When we're done, we'll have a contest."

"Yeah!" Barnaby said. "Come on, Beauregard."

The King and Queen smiled at the kids, then carried away the bowls.

Babette watched the others for a minute. After deciding that no one really needed her help, she slipped out of the room to look for Beth. Babette had a theory about the tall girl who'd told them so many lies. She hoped to find her alone.

Babette wandered through the Palace's hallways, looking at the splendid rooms. Many of them had been converted into classrooms. Several were full of bookshelves. She found a large, well-furnished gymnasium. Apparently the King and Queen believed kids should exercise their bodies as well as their minds.

Thinking that perhaps Beth had returned to the Dungeon, Babette took the elevator to the lowest level. She opened the door to the Dungeon and peered inside. "Beth?" The room was empty. The door to the Dungeon could be opened from the outside, but not the inside.

"Pete, Pete? Is that you?" a voice said. "Oh, dear. Oh, my goodness. Young lady, the Palace is closed today! What are you doing here?"

It was a tall, thin woman. "I am Babette," the French girl said politely. "A friend of Beth and Biff's." The woman had her hair in her bun; she wore a pair of small, round glasses. Her nose was long and sharp.

"Oh, well, I see. I thought you might be one of the trespassers. Are they in there? It's all a mistake, you see." The tall, bony woman peered into the Dungeon. "No? They must have gone home. I hope they are unharmed. And that poor cat. He was a very nice fellow, unusually intelligent for a cat. I came all the way down here to set them free. But they seem to have gotten out on their own." The tall, thin woman sneezed loudly, then dabbed her nose with a tissue, which she removed from a large purse. "You haven't seen a man in armor, have you? The Guard of Spelling?"

Babette smiled graciously, "You must be the Duchess of Rules. I am delighted to meet you, Madame."

The Duchess sneezed again. "I'm coming down with a cold. Or it could be that cat. I'm very fond of cats, but they make me sneeze. I don't sneeze when I am with cats, but soon after they leave me, I begin to sneeze. That doesn't make any sense, does it? My life never makes any sense. That is why I love rules. Rules make beautiful sense. It is just that...oh, I don't know." She looked around vaguely. "You haven't seen him then? The Guard?"

"Does he wear a helmet that looks rather like a pie plate?"

"Yes, exactly! You have seen him then! Where is he? Do you know?"

"I haven't any idea where he is. I met him hours ago. He was quite rude to me and my friends."

"Oh, dear. Was he? The poor man. I hope you won't hold that against him. He means well, but he's had a head injury, you see, and he's not the same. Not what he was once. He needs me to care for him, and that is why I must find him right away. Before he puts any more kids into the Dungeon."

"I am looking for Beth," Babette said. "Have you seen her?"

"Because it is all my fault, very much my fault." The Duchess began to move off down the corridor, looking for the Guard. "Pete? Where are you, Pete?"

Babette called after her, "Madame, I said, do you know where Beth is?"

"Look in her bedroom," the Duchess cried. "Room number four-fifteen, fourth floor." The tall, thin woman wandered around a corner and disappeared. Her head reappeared momentarily, "Be careful of the dog!" The Duchess vanished.

Babette took the elevator to the fourth floor. She found room number four-fifteen. On its door was a sign that read PRIVATE. Babette knocked gently on the door. When there was no answer, she knocked again, quite loudly. "Beth? Are you in there? It's Babette!" No one answered. Babette tried the doorknob and found the door unlocked. She opened it and found a bedroom. There was a long, narrow bed covered with an attractive quilt. There were lots of books and plants, a big comfortable armchair, and a stereo with a pile of CDs. "Beth?"

Babette took a step into the room. Beth was nowhere to be seen. Babette was just about to leave when she noticed that on one of the shelves was a row of notebooks. They did not look like story books, but like the sort of books that are full of blank pages that you can fill with drawings and writing. The backs of the books were numbered. Out of curiosity, Babette took down the first of the books, the one marked with a large red numeral 1.

On the cover of the book, in large purple handwritten letters, was the title, "Beth's Private Book, Vol. 1."

Babette opened the book's cover and on the first page read:

THIS BOOK IS PRIVATE!!!!!

NO ADMITTANCE WITHOUT PERMISSION!

ALL TRESPASSERS WILL BE PROSECUTED!!!

BIFF, THIS MEANS YOU!!!!

Feeling guilty that she had opened the book, Babette blushed and closed the cover.

Behind her, Babette heard a low growl.

Babette turned. There, blocking the entire doorway, was the enormous dog that had carried off Barnaby. It had its head turned and was looking at her out of the side of its eyes. Its mouth was open slightly, enough that Babette could see the dog's long, dangerous-looking teeth.

Babette carefully put the book back on the shelf beside all the other similar books. The huge beast took a step closer to her. Its long tongue appeared, licked its chops, and then disappeared.

Do not panic, Babette thought. Above all, do not panic. She remembered that Biff had told them that this dog was once a trained rescue dog.

Speaking in a very calm and soothing voice, Babette said, "Monsieur Woof, how nice to see you. I wonder if you could help me. I am looking for Beth. Do you know where she is?"

Woof made another low growl. He took another step closer to Babette. His lips drew back, exposing a little more of his teeth.

"Monsieur Woof, I do not wish to be carried by the seat of my pants. Would you be so kind as to give me a ride on your back? I would much appreciate it."

The huge dog took a long stride. He was now directly in front of Babette. He sniffed her thoughtfully, then suddenly turned around as if to leave the room. Woof took a step, then stopped and looked back over his shoulder at Babette. He made a little yelp.

In one swift motion, Babette leapt onto the back of the enormous hound. "Monsieur Woof," she said, "you are a fine gentle dog. Now, take me to your mistress."

Woof carried Beth down several long corridors, then came to a stop in front of a door marked Computer Lab. Babette said, "Thank you, Monsieur Woof. Is this the place?"

The dog barked, affirmatively.

Babette leapt off, pushed open the door, and peered into the room. The dog trotted away. The room was full of computers, at least twenty of them. Beth was leaning forward, gazing into one of the glowing screens, and typing like mad on the keyboard.

Babette entered the room and cleared her throat. Beth did not seem to hear her. The French girl took several more steps until she was only a few feet from Beth and then said, "Mademoiselle Beth?"

The tall girl jumped straight up in her chair and said, "Whoa!" She whirled around and stared at Babette. "You scared me!"

Babette took one step backward. "Mademoiselle Beth, I have been searching for you. I apologize for intruding. May I speak to you?"

Beth glanced back at her screen for a moment as if she did not like to quit writing, then said, "Shoot."

"Mademoiselle Beth, I have a confession. I trespassed."

"You what?"

"While looking for you, I entered your room."

"Yeah?" Beth cocked an eyebrow. "You didn't take anything, I hope."

"But of course not!" Babette hung her head. "I did one bad deed. I snooped."

Beth leaned back in her chair and gave Babette a long look. "Yeah? So what'd you find?"

"I saw the long row of your journals; I opened one of them, the first one. I did not read beyond the first page, but you see—I am a trespasser and an invader of your privacy. I've come to beg your pardon."

"You sound like a seriously bad person," Beth said. It was hard to tell if she was kidding. "Hope you're not on your way to reform school."

"Mademoiselle Beth, I hope you will not laugh at me, but I have a theory about you. My belief is that you are a writer!"

Beth seemed a little surprised.

"I think that writers must develop their imaginations, and that is why you told us all those stories. I also know that writers must know as much as possible, and that is why you are always reading. Tell me, please, am I right? Are you a writer?"

"So how come you want to know?"

"Because I am a writer too—a poet!"

"You're not mad at me for telling whoppers?"

"No, Mademoiselle, I am not angry. I thought your stories were most amusing—even if they were not true."

"Ha!" Beth stuck out her hand. "Let's shake. I've never had a friend from France before!"

"You *are* a writer then. I knew it!" Babette took Beth's hand and gave it a friendly shake. "I have rarely met a writer so young."

Beth explained, "What I like to write is mysteries." She tapped the screen of her computer. "I'm writing a message to some e-mail pals. I'm on a listserve. Do you know what that is?"

"Something on the Internet?"

"We're like a club of young mystery writers; we all write back and forth all the time. If you send a message to the listserve, then it goes to all the members, so everybody can read everybody else's stuff. We're called the Mysterians. Cool name, don't you think?"

"What a good idea, a community of writers!"

"Well, if you're gonna write, it's a good idea to have an audience of people who read your stuff. How else are you gonna find out if you're any good?"

"You send your stories back and forth? You give each other advice?"

"Sure, and anything else: jokes, gossip, what we think about movies and music—all kinds of stuff."

"I believe it is very good for writers to write, the more writing the better."

"You sound just like the King and Queen," Beth made a funny face. "I shouldn't have said they were cruel. It was like a bad joke. I just thought it would be funny to pretend such good people were mean. They're just about the nicest guardians a kid could have. They're great teachers, too. When it comes to writing, they always say the same thing you just said. Writing is a skill. If you want to get better at it, do a lot of it. Plus, get other people to read your stuff and give you advice, help you find your mistakes. Stuff like that. What I like about the Mysterians is that they are all about my age. They're interested in the same stuff I am—mystery stories. They're really great at finding my spelling mistakes, plus they give me lots of other writing advice: how to make my characters more interesting, how to keep the reader interested."

"And does Biff want to be a writer too?"

"Biff? You kidding? He never writes, if he can get out of it."

"And so he must work on his spelling."

"Exactly. I guess the King and Queen are right. If you really want to get good at spelling, you should do a lot of writing. Write every day if possible."

"And get others, as you say, 'to read your stuff.'"

"Right! Hey, Babette, can I tell you something? I sure like those black clothes you've got on. Plus those sunglasses. Totally cool."

"I much admire your braid, Beth, and the way you toss it when you are thinking. And your height. It must be wonderful to be so tall!"

Beth grinned. She stuck her long legs out in front of her and crossed them at the ankles. "So this is why you came looking for me, huh? To find out if I'm a writer?"

Babette nodded. "May I sit down?"

"You had to ask?" Beth pointed at a chair.

Babette seated herself. She scooted the chair a little closer to Beth. "I had another reason to seek you out, mademoiselle. I desire your help."

"My help? Well, just ask."

"I wish to solve a mystery!"

Beth drew in her long legs and sat up straight in her chair. "What mystery?"

"A mystery associated with this splendid Palace, mademoiselle."

Beth's eyebrows shot up, then lowered. "This Palace? Take my word for it; I've lived here for years, and there are definitely no mysteries to this place. At first, it seems cool, a free school that looks like a Palace. But after you get used to it, this Palace is so normal, it's boring!" Beth rolled her eyes to indicate how totally dull the Palace was in her opinion.

"It is easy to imagine that what we know is not interesting and exciting," Babette said. "Sometimes it takes an outsider, a stranger, to make us realize that life is full of mysteries and love stories!"

"Love stories?" One side of Beth's mouth rose up in a sarcastic grin. "Here? You've gotta be kidding me."

"I do love a good mystery story but, of all the forms of stories, my favorite is the love story. Here, at your so-called boring Palace, there is a wonderful mystery and a sad love story."

Beth folded her long, slender arms and gave Babette another long, doubtful look. "So what are you waiting for, what's the big mystery? Who's in love?"

"The Duchess of Rules and the mysterious Guard of Spelling, mademoiselle. They are the lovers; they are the chief characters of the mystery story."

Beth unfolded her arms and grimaced. "Oh, them." She squinted at Babette in disappointment. "For a second, I thought you really had something interesting."

Babette's voice became more urgent. "The King and Queen told us the entire story. Once upon a time, the Guard, Pete, was on the verge of proposing, then...what? Something happened! But, what was it? And now, he has forgotten everything! What a disaster! Consider how sad it is. Consider the feelings of the unfortunate Duchess Ruthie. Is there no way to help them?"

Beth tugged on her braid. "I guess I'm so used to them, I sort of forgot about all that. It *is* kind of mysterious, isn't it?" She looked at Babette and fingered her braid.

"The King and Queen were at the door; they heard the murmur of voices, then..."

"A loud thump!" Beth said excitedly. "Hey, you know what? There were two thumps! I remember the King telling me that the first time he told the story." She reached out and slapped Babette on the knee. "First a thump, then a second louder one. Thump, then THUMP!"

The two girls looked into one another's excited eyes.

The computer let out a loud beep.

Startled by the sound, Babette jumped a little. "What is it? What is that beep?"

"I must have a new email." Beth swiveled in her chair to look at the screen of her computer. "Hey, it's an instant message from Biff!"

Babette and Beth leaned into the screen to read the message:

HEY, BETH AND BABETTE, WE'VE LEARNED ALL THE FIEND-ISHLY HARD WORDS. BEAUREGARD AND I ARE GOING TO HAVE A CONTEST. COME AT ONCE! WE'RE WAITING FOR YOU!

SINCERELY,

BIFF, BRIDGET, BEAUREGARD, AND BARNABY.

Aa Bb Cc Dd Ee Ff Gg Hh Ii Jj

Exercises for Chapter 9

These are the last twelve of the list of Fiendishly Hard Words. If you can learn how to spell these dozen words, you will have mastered the entire list and will be ready for the Review Test.

AGAIN—don't misspell it AGIN. This word has GAIN in it.

AROUND—don't misspell it AROWND. If you know how to spell the shape ROUND, you know how to spell AROUND, but don't forget it is one word, not two.

DIFFERENT—remember those two Fs! Don't forget the ER in the middle: DIFF–ER–ENT.

ESPECIALLY—remember that it contains the word SPECIAL and has two Ls: E–SPECIAL–LY.

FAVORITE—don't forget that O in the middle; don't forget the silent E at the end: it's the word FAVOR with ITE tacked on the end.

FRIENDS—IE in the middle; don't forget the D at the end. Don't misspell it FRENDS or FRENS. Here's a good clue to help you remember how to spell it: FRI–ENDs to the END.

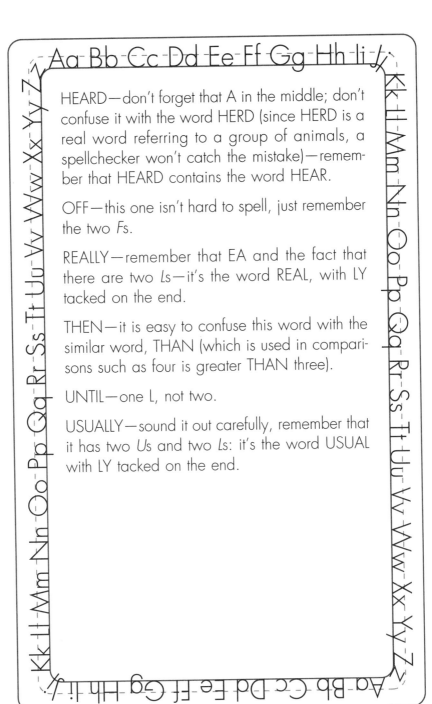

Aa Bb Cc Dd Ee Ff Gg Hh Ii Jj

HEARD—don't forget that A in the middle; don't confuse it with the word HERD (since HERD is a real word referring to a group of animals, a spellchecker won't catch the mistake)—remember that HEARD contains the word HEAR.

OFF—this one isn't hard to spell, just remember the two *F*s.

REALLY—remember that EA and the fact that there are two *L*s—it's the word REAL, with LY tacked on the end.

THEN—it is easy to confuse this word with the similar word, THAN (which is used in comparisons such as four is greater THAN three).

UNTIL—one L, not two.

USUALLY—sound it out carefully, remember that it has two *U*s and two *L*s: it's the word USUAL with LY tacked on the end.

Aa Bb Cc Dd Ee Ff Gg Hh Ii Jj

Find and correct the spelling mistakes. The number of mistakes is in parentheses at the end of the sentences.

1. "Gett awf the bed!" Mrs. Smith yelled at her rhinoceros. (2)

2. "Turn of that light," said the elegant vampire, "I prefer the darkness."(1)

3. Untill I was twelve, I reelly hated green vegetables. (2)

4. He yelled at his teacher and at the principal, than he realy got into trouble! (2)

5. I'd rather take a shower then I would a bath. (1)

6. Coach's faverite football players are smart, but he specialy likes Joe. (2)

7. I usally like pancakes for breakfast, but today I'd like something diferent—lobster! (2)

8. Have you hurd what her faverit dog did? (2)

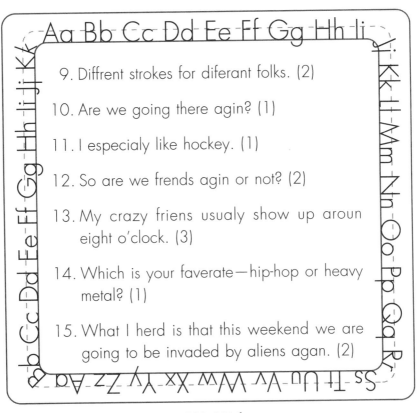

9. Diffrent strokes for diferant folks. (2)

10. Are we going there agin? (1)

11. I especialy like hockey. (1)

12. So are we frends agin or not? (2)

13. My crazy friens usualy show up aroun eight o'clock. (3)

14. Which is your faverate—hip-hop or heavy metal? (1)

15. What I herd is that this weekend we are going to be invaded by aliens agan. (2)

see pages 250–251 for answers

Review Test—The List of Fiendishly Hard Words

If you have read the previous chapters and done all the exercises so far, you are ready to take this test. Don't freak out if you still make some mistakes! As we keep saying, even excellent writers make some spelling mistakes. The most important thing is to improve, learn new words and ways to catch and correct your mistakes. The answers are at the back of the book.

Find and correct all the spelling errors in the following sentences. Some sentences have more than one mistake. The number of spelling mistakes will be in the parentheses at the end.

1. Thare sure are alot of monsters in this swamp. (2)

2. I will take too of those doughnuts, please. (1)

3. Too get two they're house, drive down that road. (3)

4. The dog wagged it's tail. (1)

5. Its about time you guys showed up. (1)

6. Becuz you lost the ticket, I dont get to go. (2)

7. There probbly going to be here on Eester. (3)

8. Thay think your not coming. (2)

9. We spent are Chrismas in Colorado. (2)

10. Finaly, she got awf the phone. (2)

11. Whare are you going this Haloween? (2)

12. The car did'nt stop untill it crashed. (2)

13. Are you going to by that comic book or just read it? (1)

14. Let's get reely serious about winning the next game. (2)

15. She ran down the steps, than turned right. (1)

16. Usally were at home by 8 P.M. (2)

17. Sumtimes we whent north, other times south. (2)

18. Did you go thru the tunnel? (1)

19. Witch of these colors does'nt match? (2)

20. Have you herd your favrit song yet? (2)

21. I can't beleeve you fell for that agin! (2)

22. I could except the fact that you failed the test accept for the fact that you also cheated. (2)

23. Evrything about this room seems difrent. (2)

24. Those people we're all ways getting lost, especialy on Saterday. (4)

25. We all ways take our frends evrywhere we go. (3)

26. May be every body else is going to that party, but your not! (3)

27. He did'nt no what he should do next. (2)

28. Some one said he went to the resteraunt with her. (2)

29. Theres only one thing I like about they're resterant—the spicy food. (3)

see page 251 for answers

Chapter 10:
Biff vs. Beauregard

PRINCIPAL and PRINCIPLE are two words that people confuse all the time...read on.

As Babette and Beth took the elevator up to Biff's room in the Tower, they talked excitedly about the mystery of the Guard's amnesia. Something had happened to the man when he was alone with the Duchess. Something had changed him from a fairly sensible man who was about to propose to the woman he loved into a nutty guy who dressed up like Don Quixote and imagined he was the grandly important Guard of Spelling— and completely forgot that he was ever in love with the Duchess!

"There were two thumps," Beth said, "not just one! I'm sure that's what the King said right after it happened. The second one was louder. Thump, then THUMP!"

"Something hit poor Monsieur Pete over the head," Babette said, "do you think? And that caused thump number one?"

Beth nodded. "Then he keeled over and his body must've hit the floor hard. That was the second thump, the loud one. Thump, then THUMP!"

"It makes sense," Babette agreed.

Beth looked shocked. "She hit him! She smacked him over the head and knocked him out! Maybe with a baseball bat!"

Babette expressed a little doubt, "Although I do not know Madame Ruthie very well at all, she does not seem to me the sort of lady who would do something so, so..."

Beth covered her mouth and laughed. "I guess she wouldn't. She doesn't even own a baseball bat." She grinned. "Well, it was just a thought!"

Babette looked at her, "You don't think she would?"

"Nah, I guess not. Aunt Ruthie gets a little peeved from time to time. She bites her lip and turns red in the face, and she even stamps her foot. She's a bit of a nitwit, but she'd never hit anybody. Besides, she was dying for him to propose. Why would she smack him?"

"She surely loves him?"

"I'd be lying if I said any different. She's crazy about him."

"And he was definitely about to propose?"

Beth tapped her chin with her index finger. "I see what you mean. Maybe if he went in there and told her he was never going to marry her, he broke her heart. So she got mad and smacked him. That would be a great theory, except he told the Queen all about how he was going to propose. He even asked for advice about how to do it! He went in there with that exact plan, to propose. The King and Queen went to her room with him. They were right outside the door, trying to listen."

Babette looked up at the ceiling of the elevator. "The one time I saw her, your Duchess, she was wandering the halls of the Palace, looking for him. I believe she loves him very much." Babette looked down at her feet. "Hmm...."

"What?" Beth looked eagerly at the French girl. "You just thought of something."

"The Duchess told me that it is her fault—the Guard's condition. She was coming to let us out of the Dungeon. She said, 'It's my fault, it's all my fault.' I am sure she said that."

Beth looked her in the eye. "Then she *did* hit him!"

"You think so?"

Beth tugged her braid. "Nah, I just can't believe it. It's impossible! But it seems like the only explanation." She winked at Babette. "What a great mystery!" She pointed at the top of the elevator where an electronic display showed the floors, "Hey, we're almost there. Sorry about this elevator; it's the slowest one in the world."

"Oh, it is not so bad. You should ride some of the ones we have in Paris."

The elevator came to a stop and its door opened quietly.

Bridget was standing in the doorway to Biff's room. She gave them a hard look and put her finger to her lips. "Ssshh!" Standing in front of Biff's room with her jaw stuck out, Bridget looked a little like a guard dog.

They came up to her. "Has the contest started?"

"About time you guys showed up!" Bridget lowered her voice and drew them a little ways from the door. "The King and Queen made up a test for them to take. They're taking it right now!"

Babette peeked into the room.

Biff and Beauregard were seated at a table. Both of them were hard at work taking their spelling test. From time to time, the cat gnawed on his pencil. Biff let out a loud sigh, then frowned ferociously. Beauregard wiggled his whiskers and lashed the air with his tail. The cat looked up at the ceiling.

"Done!" Biff said. He laid down his pencil. "Who wants to check it?"

The King nudged the Queen. "Dear, why don't I check the boy's work—and you can check the cat's."

"Very good, darling," the Queen said.

The King took Biff's piece of paper and began to inspect it carefully.

The Queen approached the cat. "Beauregard, are you fin-ished? Do you need more time?"

Beauregard wrote down one last word, then sighed loudly and pushed his piece of paper toward the Queen. "Go on— I did my best."

The Queen picked up the test paper and squinted at it. "Oh dear," she murmured, "I do need new glasses."

The King made a mark on Biff's paper. The Queen circled something on Beauregard's.

"I can't watch," Beauregard said. He covered his eyes with his paws. Biff kicked the ankle of one of his shoes with the toe of the other.

The King made another mark; the Queen circled another word.

"Done," said the King.

"Finished," said the Queen.

Biff stood up. Beauregard raised his head. Beth, Babette, Bridget, and Barnaby circled around the King and Queen.

"Who won?!" Bridget yelled.

"Biff, my boy," the King said, "you did very well. Fine job." He gave the boy an encouraging smile. "I am proud of you!"

"How many did he miss?!" Bridget yelled.

"Only two," the King said.

"And what about Beauregard?" Bridget asked the Queen. Since she had coached Biff, Bridget could hardly conceal the fact she hoped Biff had done better than Beauregard.

The Queen cleared her throat. She held up the piece of paper. "Beauregard," she gazed fondly at the large cat, "you are a wonderful speller. Why, I've rarely seen better spelling! This is practically perfect!"

"But how many did he miss?" Bridget cried. She yanked off her baseball cap, slapped it against her hip, then pulled it back on her head. "I can't stand the suspense! Who won?"

"Beauregard, you got almost all of them right. You missed— let me look again." The queen adjusted her glasses and peered again at the piece of paper. "Only two."

"Two?" Biff asked.

"Two?" Beauregard said. "You mean we tied?"

"You both won," the King said. "What do you think, Mom? Take them both to a baseball game?"

"Take them *all* to a baseball game," the Queen said. "What a lovely idea! We'll go this very weekend!"

Biff and Beauregard grinned at each other.

"That's the best I ever did in my life on a spelling test," Biff said. "Only two wrong!"

Beauregard said, "That's the best I ever did!"

"Great job for both of you!" Barnaby said.

Bridget cleared her throat loudly. She crossed her arms and stuck out her jaw. "Tie breaker."

"Excuse me, dear," the Queen said, "what was that?"

Bridget stepped closer to the cat and Biff. "PRINCIPLE and PRINCIPAL. Biff, that is your tie-breaker word. There are two kinds. The PRINCIPAL of a school, and a PRINCIPLE of life, a good rule you live by. Biff, spell PRINCIPAL—the one that means the person who runs a school."

"Bridget, dear," the Queen said, "there's really no need..."

Biff waved off the Queen. "I can get this one." He licked his lips; he rubbed his hands together. A long time ago, he'd learned these words. There was a cool trick that helped you remember. What was it? Bam! It came back to him. PRINCI— PAL! That was it! The PRINCIPAL is your PAL! The other kind was spelled PRINCI—PLE. Just to have a little fun, Biff sighed. He hung his head and let his shoulders slump as if he was really getting depressed. "Wow, this is really tough."

Bridget looked gloomy. Beauregard perked up and waved his tail happily. Was it possible that he, Beauregard, the worst speller in New York, was going to win the spelling contest? Beauregard was never afraid of a competition. He loved to win and hated to lose, but never in his life had he dreamed of winning a spelling contest. The kid hasn't got a chance, he thought happily. I've got to try not to gloat when I win.

"P–R–I–N–C–I." Biff said slowly. He squinted his eyes. He rubbed his chin. "P."

Bridget leaned forward. The King and Queen leaned forward. It was so quiet you could hear a flea sneeze.

"A–L!" Biff yelled triumphantly. "P–R–I–N–C–I–P–A–L!"

The cat snorted. "Wrong!" he said loudly.

"Right!" Bridget yelled. "Absolutely perfect."

"He's right," the Queen said.

"Congratulations, Biff!" the King said.

Beauregard sat down on the floor and tried not to show his disgust.

Bridget turned to the cat. "Beauregard, you ready?"

"I dislike contests," the cat said. "I think competition is silly."

Bridget grinned. "FEBRUARY."

The cat stiffened. His tail stood straight up until it resembled an exclamation point, then it drooped to the floor, then it came up again and waved from side to side as if it was a sort of metronome.

"February." Beauregard said the word slowly, sounding it out in his head and visualizing the letters. "F–E–B." He half-closed his eyes and looked at Bridget. She had her arms crossed. Her face was blank—her poker face. Impossible to read her. Quickly, Beauregard spelled the name of the month exactly the way it sounds, "F–E–B–U–A–R–Y!"

Biff looked at Bridget; she was grinning from ear to ear. "That's right, isn't it?" he asked.

"That's 100 percent wrong!" Bridget yelled. "He left out the R in the middle!" She ran to Biff and hoisted the handsome kid's arm into the air as if he was a boxer and had just won a heavyweight championship fight. "Biff's the winner!" she yelled. "Hooray for the Spelling Champion of the Universe!"

"Way to go, Biff!" Barnaby grinned at Biff. "Give me a high-five!" The two kids smacked their hands together.

"Wow," Biff said, "that's the first spelling contest I ever won in my whole life."

Bridget told Beauregard, "Sorry, buddy, it's spelled F–E–B–R–U–A–R–Y. It's one of those really weird words—it's got that silent R right after FEB." She patted the cat on the head. "Tough luck, Beauregard. No hard feelings, huh?"

The cat hissed and pulled away from Bridget. "That's it," Beauregard said. His voice was cold and furious. "Never again in my life will I spell another word. I hate spelling. I hate writing. I hate contests!" The cat turned his back on all of them, walked into a corner and sat down, as if it was his intention to sit there in that corner for the rest of his nine lives.

Bridget's mouth fell open. "Hey, pal, I didn't mean to...wow. I never meant to hurt your feelings! I'm really sorry."

She looked helplessly at the others.

Babette came up to the cat and tried to soothe him. "Monsieur Beauregard, you are a fine speller. Superb."

"That's right!" Biff said. "Beauregard, I mean it. If you hadn't helped me, I never could have learned all those words. It was pure luck that I knew that PRINCIPLE/PRINCIPAL one! See, the trick is to remember 'The PRINCIPAL is your PAL.' It ends with P–A–L."

"Pure luck is right," Beth nodded her head vigorously. "He's my brother, and I know. Beauregard, no kidding, Biff just got lucky because she picked one of the few words he knows. I think you are a first-rate speller!" Beth scratched her head. "Especially for a cat."

Beauregard had been getting calmer. As the others had complimented him, he had gradually softened and had even begun to think that maybe he shouldn't have gotten so mad after all.

"For an animal, wow," Beth continued, "you must be the world's champ. I mean, except for old Woof, I bet you are the best speller in the entire animal kingdom!"

The cat turned around slowly until he was looking directly at Beth. "What was that you said?"

Barnaby waved his hands wildly at Beth, signaling her not to speak.

Bridget groaned.

"Oh, no," Babette murmured.

"Really," Beth said, "except for our dog Woof, you're the best. I mean it!" She nodded at the cat as if she was giving him a great compliment.

Beauregard stood to his feet. He arched his back as high as it would go. The hair on his back rose straight up until he seemed to turn into a giant cat. "The honor of all cats has been called into question," he said. "You all heard it. I demand...," Beauregard smiled his most ferocious cat-smile, "a contest."

Exercises for Chapter 10

Here are some more tricky words. They are all very easy to misspell!

EFFECT, AFFECT—it is very easy to confuse these two words. Most of the time AFFECT is a verb, and EFFECT is a noun. To AFFECT means *to act upon,* or *to influence.* The team doctor wondered how the flu would AFFECT the star player's performance. The EFFECT of the flu turned out to be that the star player could not play at all. But just to keep us spellers confused, sometimes EFFECT is a verb. The word is not used as a verb very often but, when it is, EFFECT means *to bring about,* or *to achieve* or *accomplish.* The doctor EFFECTED a cure.

FEBRUARY—the second month. Easy to misspell because of that weird silent R after FEB. It is spelled as if you should pronounce it Feb–roo–ary!

FOR, FOUR, FORTH, FOURTH, FORTY—it is easy to get confused about how to spell these words. FOR is the preposition and is easy to spell. Just try not to get the preposition FOR confused with the number FOUR! FORTH means *forward* or *onward* and is not used a great deal in modern times. FOURTH means *next after third*, or *one of four equal parts of a thing*. It is easy to remember since it starts with the word FOUR. The word FORTY is tricky because it is NOT the word FOUR plus TY. Don't stick in that extra U!

LABORATORY—like February, it is weird since it contains a silent letter. We pronounce it LAB–RUH–TORY, so it is easy to misspell it LABRATORY. Try to remember that it begins with the word LABOR. "Scientists LABOR in the LABOR–ATORY."

LOSE, LOOSE, LOSS—The word LOSE is irregular; the O has an OO sound. "I hope we don't LOSE the game." The typical mistake is to write LOOSE instead of LOSE. The S in LOOSE is hissed so it rhymes with goose (the cows got LOOSE from the pasture). LOSS is probably the easiest of these words since it is spelled exactly as it sounds, with a double S. "That was the worst LOSS we had all season."

Aa Bb Cc Dd Ee Ff Gg Hh Ii

PRINCIPAL—this one is easy to confuse with the sound-alike word PRINCIPLE. PRINCIPAL means *first in importance* or *chief; the head of some institution like a school* or *a capital sum of money that is lent or invested.* If you want to write about the boss of your school, one helpful trick is to remember the saying that Biff remembered, "The PRINCIPAL is your PAL." Even if it isn't true, the saying can help you remember the correct way to spell PRINCIPAL! PRINCIPLE means *a fundamental truth or law, a personal code of conduct.* An honorable person lives by high PRINCIPLES.

Find the misspelled words and correct them. The total number of errors is noted in the parentheses at the end of the sentences.

1. The way that Michael Jordan sticks out his tongue doesn't effect the way he shoots, but try telling him that! (1)

2. The main affect of the earth tilting away from the sun is winter. The main affect of hitting yourself for times in the head with a hammer is you get a terrible headache! (3)

3. On the last day of Febuary, the masked bandits rode fourth into the woods. (2)

4. On the Forth of July, we are all going to the fireworks show on the river. (1)

5. Miss Diego, the principle of our school, turned fourty years old today. (2)

6. The principle actor in the play is the king. (1)

7. If you guys don't make more of your free throws, we are going to loose the game. (1)

Aa Bb Cc Dd Ee Ff Gg Hh Ii Jj

8. The school board fired our principle because he was a total goofball. (1)

9. There's a hole in the fence; that's why all the pigs got lose! (1)

10. She lives by the principal of total and complete honesty—so you have to be nuts to ask her what she thinks of your clothes! (1)

11. Our worst los all year was the close one against Senior High School. We lost in the second overtime by only for points! (2)

12. Febuary is the shortest and coldest month of the year. (1)

13. The mad scientist ran into his labratory and yelled, "Now, where did I put that brain?! That's the forth time this week I've lost a brain!" (2)

14. Bring me all for of those test tubes. (1)

15. Last Febuary, our school principle was terribly effected by the lost of his beloved wife. (4)

16. If we add an ounce of sodium, what do you think will be the affect? (1)

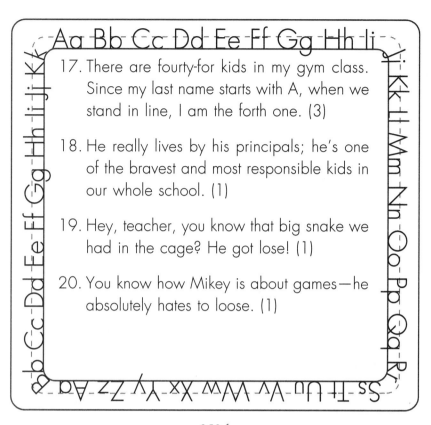

17. There are fourty-for kids in my gym class. Since my last name starts with A, when we stand in line, I am the forth one. (3)

18. He really lives by his principals; he's one of the bravest and most responsible kids in our whole school. (1)

19. Hey, teacher, you know that big snake we had in the cage? He got lose! (1)

20. You know how Mikey is about games—he absolutely hates to loose. (1)

see page 252 for answers

Chapter 11:
The Mystery

To SUCCEED in anything, you need to know how to spell SUCCEED— remember two *Cs*, two *Es*!

After the King ran off to fetch the enormous hound dog, Woof, Beauregard twitched his tail and wiggled his whiskers. He was full of nervous energy. "No dog can spell. Obviously the beast must be cheating." His tail lashed the air as if it would like to hit someone, preferably a dog. "I never have understood how you humans can possibly like dogs in the first place. How can you allow them in the house? As you know, they are likely to chew up your slippers. They nip small children and knock old people flat! Not to mention their revolting body odor! And their ear-splitting barking!" Although Beauregard did not like to admit it to his human friends, many times he'd been chased up a tree or telephone pole by some snarling, snapping dog. He hated the entire species.

Beth and Biff assured the others that Woof really could spell. "The Guard taught him," Biff explained. "He's a Wonder Dog!"

Beauregard snorted. "Wonder Dog! The very idea is absurd! What could possibly be wonderful about a dog? I don't even like to say the word! Even the sound of it is hideous. It rhymes with hog, you know. Dogs have very small brains. They cannot spell or read or speak—or do anything else worthy of respect. A dog may be a flea scratcher; he may be a yawner, a chewer, a barker, a howler, or a biter—but he cannot possibly be a good speller!"

"Wait and see." Biff nodded at the others. "Maybe Woof does have a small brain, but he's a better speller than I am."

Beth grinned crookedly. "Biff, everyone in the world is a better speller than you!"

"Not Beauregard," Biff said. Then he slapped his hand over his mouth, realizing he had said something rather unkind.

"I cannot possibly believe that...that...that DOG," Beauregard pronounced the word *dog* as if it were something so horrible that it dripped slime, "is a good speller. Of course, he is nothing of the kind. The very idea that a dog—ANY dog—could possibly be smarter than I am! Absurd! In any fair contest involving intelligence, a cat will pulverize a mere dog." Beauregard rose up on his hind legs and elevated his chin. "Why, it will be downright pitiful what happens to Woof. After he disgraces the honor of all canines, the wretched creature will live in shame. For the rest of his life, he will hang his head and walk with his tail between his legs."

As if a new idea had just occurred to him, Beauregard whirled around and glared at Barnaby. "Isn't this Woof the very monster who attacked you? The giant beast who dragged you down the Dungeon? He's the sort of beast who should be kept on a leash. He's an ogre who should be muzzled and put in a kennel, preferably the kind made out of cast iron! He should be dragged off to the Humane Society and put to sleep!"

"Oh, don't worry about that," Biff said. "He's a nice dog. He won't eat you or anything."

The very idea that Woof might eat him made Beauregard so furious his hair stood on end. He strode around Biff's room, lashing his tail and hissing. "I'll destroy him," he muttered. "I'll demoralize, astonish, and smash him! A dog who can spell better than I can! Ridiculous!"

While Beauregard fumed about the deplorable reputation of the entire dog species, Bridget and Barnaby worked on a list of new words. They would present the new words to the contestants, Beauregard and Woof. They would split up and coach them, then give them a test. It would be a great competition. Beauregard vs. Woof! Beauregard would defend the honor of all cats, and Woof would defend the honor of dogs.

"Hey, you know what? We should invite the Duchess of Rules," Bridget said. "I'd like to get a look at her. Barnaby and I have never met her."

"Why, that is an excellent idea, Bridget," the Queen agreed. "I'll go find her and ask her if she would like to watch." The Queen rose to leave the room.

Beth gave Babette a quick nudge with her elbow. "Hey, your Majesty, could we come along? Babette here needs to stretch her legs."

"Of course you can," the Queen said graciously. "I'll be glad to have some company."

As they walked through the Palace toward the quarters of the Duchess of Rules, Beth steered the conversation to the topic of the Guard. She complained that his behavior was getting worse and worse. "He's throwing bad spellers in the dungeon again. I hate to say it, your Majesty, but he's getting downright dangerous."

The Queen made a sad face. "The King will have to talk to Pete again." She looked at Babette. "He was once a fine fellow, before his…er…accident. I hope you realize that you are not seeing him at his best. The King and I are very fond of him. He's the best brother a girl could possibly have. I love him very much. To see him as he is now…well, it is all very sad."

Beth took a deep breath. "Your Majesty, I am just going to say this and get it over with. I hope you don't get mad at me. But you know what I'm like. Once I get started thinking about a mystery, I can't stop until I get to the bottom of it."

Her Majesty came to a stop in the middle of the hallway and looked thoughtfully at Beth. "A mystery, dear? What mystery would that be?"

Beth told her that she had discussed the mystery of the Guard's amnesia with Babette. "Thump, then THUMP! We figure something hit him over the head; that was the first thump. Then he crashed to the floor, and that was the second. It seems impossible, but we figure maybe the Duchess smacked him over the head!"

Babette asked, "Can it be true, your Majesty?"

The Queen drew herself to her full height; she was nearly as tall as Beth. She folded her arms and looked quite seriously into the eyes of the tall girl. "Beth, I am not at liberty to tell you the entire story. To do so would be terribly indiscreet. But I do want you to know—are you listening to me? This is very serious."

"I'm all ears!"

"The Duchess Ruthie did not bang that poor man over the head. Don't you dare imagine she did. You'd better not start a rumor like that!" She reached out and took hold of Beth's hand. "Have you told this story to anyone else, dear?"

"Only to Babette."

The Queen looked carefully at Babette. "It is not true, not a word of it. Babette, the Duchess may be a bit eccentric, but she is good through and through. She would never hurt poor old Pete, not intentionally. She would not hurt a fly!"

After looking carefully at both of them to be sure they saw how important she felt all this was, the Queen said, "I want your word, Beth—and yours, Babette. You will not tell anyone that the Duchess hit my poor brother over the head!"

Babette blushed. She felt a little ashamed of herself. "I am terribly sorry, Madame."

"Me, too," Beth hung her head. She reached up and played with her braid. "But I sure wish I knew the whole story."

"Ahem!" Behind them, someone loudly cleared her throat. "Then it is time I told them, your Majesty!"

They all whirled around and there was the Duchess! She was staring directly at them.

How long had she been standing behind them? Beth and Babette felt terribly embarrassed. Had the Duchess heard every single thing they'd said?

The Duchess's thin lips were pressed together; her arms were crossed.

"Oh, Ruthie," the Queen said, "I hope they didn't hurt your feelings. I'm sure these girls did not mean to!"

"That is quite all right, your Majesty," the Duchess held up her hand. "It is time I told someone besides you. Beth, since you live here with us, it is time you heard the entire story."

"You don't have to say a word, Ruthie," the Queen said, "not unless you want to!"

Babette stepped back slightly. "Madame, I do not live here; I have no claim on you at all. If you would like to be left alone with your friends, with Beth and her Majesty, I will go away at once!" Babette was ordinarily an extremely polite person, and she felt just awful about talking behind the Duchess's back.

"That is quite all right," The Duchess sniffed loudly. "It is time I told the whole story. Never mind, your Majesty, I want to do this. And you—is it Babette?—I've forgotten your name."

"It is Babette, Madame," the French girl made a little curtsy. "I am very glad to meet you."

"Girls," the Duchess said, "you see before you a victim of pride. Of secrecy and gravity!" She turned and opened a door. "Come into this room. Sit down with me. I will tell you the entire story."

A minute later, all of them were seated around a small table. Before any of the others could speak, the Duchess held up her hands. "Please, no interruptions. This is not an easy story to tell. Pete's condition—you girls are right. It *is* all my fault." The Duchess removed her round glasses and peered at them to see if they were clean. Discovering a slight smear on one lens, she pulled out a folded up tissue from the sleeve of her dress, unfolded it, and polished the lens of her spectacles. Then she refolded the tissue and tucked it back into her sleeve. "Simplified spelling. Rationalized spelling. It was my passion. My cause. I could not tell Pete about it. He loves English as it is, you see, and will not tolerate any changes. But I thought I knew better. Such was my pride. I thought I could save the world by simplifying spelling!" The Duchess paused. "Even now, even after the disaster, I sometimes think how much better we would all be, all of us who speak and write in English, if only the language, and especially the spelling, were simplified. Do you speak any other languages, Babette?"

Babette did not like to brag, but in fact she spoke many different languages. "A few," she said politely.

"In some languages, for example, Spanish, if you hear a word pronounced, then you can spell it. If you see a word written down, you can say it correctly. But this is not the case in English. If only the language could be simplified!" She looked up at Babette and Beth. "I secretly started a dictionary—a Dictionary of Rationalized Spelling. A perfectly huge book." She sniffed rather proudly. "As big as the New York City phonebook!" Her cheeks turned pink. "I spent years putting it together. Through the Internet, I am in touch with many other people who share my desire to reform our language, to simplify spelling! It has been a lifelong hobby, a vocation, a passion." Her eyes blazed, then suddenly grew dim. She looked down and sighed.

"The God of Love, I sometimes think, has a curious sense of humor. I fell in love with Pete, and he with me. We were in agreement about all sorts of things. But he was not reasonable, not at all, when it came to spelling. He is a traditionalist." She sighed. "I thought it a flaw in his character, but perhaps over time I could cure him of his prejudice against Simplified Spelling. I could enlist him in our great cause!"

Beth leaned forward. "What happened, Duchess? We know Pete came to see you. We know he was going to propose. What happened?"

"I was working on my dictionary when he knocked on the door and called out my name. I am afraid that I panicked. What if he saw my dictionary? What if it made him so mad, he decided not to propose? I thought—I must hide it! Hide the dictionary! I tried to put it under a chair, but it would not fit. Too fat! He knocked again. 'Ruthie, you in there?' I put the fat manuscript up on a narrow shelf out of sight. Well, most of it was out of sight. If only it had not grown so big! I opened the door and let him in. And that was the happiest moment of my life. In came Pete. He loved me, and I loved him. I forgot all about my stupid dictionary. Oh, you should have seen him. Dear man! He was terribly embarrassed. He is sweet and kind, but he is a bit stiff when it comes to the tender emotions. He tried to speak his mind. He turned red.

He huffed and he puffed. Finally, he gave up all hope of being dignified. He fell to one knee; he took my hand in his, and proposed!" The Duchess took off her glasses again and dabbed her eyes with the tissue. "Oh, it was the most beautiful thing. A man's face—even when it is only a plain, honest face—when in love, a man's face becomes radiant. I said yes, of course. I kissed his hand and said, 'Yes, yes, yes!'"

"Oh, Ruthie," the Queen said kindly.

"What happened?" Beth yelled.

"He leapt to his feet, that is what happened. He jumped for joy. And his head collided with the shelf. The dictionary fell. It hit the poor man in the head and knocked him silly. He fell over like a tree falling. He and the dictionary hit the floor at the same time. Oh, I thought I'd killed him! It was the most awful, the most terrible and tragic event of my entire life."

The Queen rose, went to the Duchess, sat beside her, and put an arm around her. "There, there, honey," she said kindly. "It's all in the past."

"I relive that moment every day of my life," the Duchess said sadly. "Ever since that day, he has suffered from amnesia. He has never recalled that he was proposing to me—or that I accepted. He's forgotten that his name is Pete. He believes he is indeed the Guard of Spelling. When anyone tries to tell him the truth about what happened that day—and girls, I have tried, take my word for it—the poor man becomes so agitated, he turns red in the face and then faints dead away. And when he awakens, he is the Guard of Spelling. And he never remembers we were in love."

"Now, now," the Queen patted Ruthie's hand.

"He is stricter than ever about spelling. That is why he throws bad spellers in the Dungeon."

"And that is why," the Queen said, "we take care of him to this day. Girls, I hope you understand at last."

Beth looked at Babette, and Babette looked at Beth. Neither of them said anything, but both of them had the same thought. Somehow or other, they had to straighten all this out. They had to restore the Guard's memory!

"Come along now, everyone," the Queen rose to her feet. "We were looking for you, Ruthie. We are going to have an exciting competition. Woof is going to compete in a spelling contest with that wonderful talking cat, Beauregard. Come and watch!"

Exercises for Chapter 11

These are some of the tricky words that Bridget and Barnaby picked out for the big contest.

BUSY—this is the only word in which U is pronounced as a short I. Don't spell it BIZZY.

CHOIR—this is one of our weirdest words. Don't spell it QUIRE or KWIRE, think of this, "A CHOIR sings a series of *CHORDS*."

DIAMOND—don't forget the A. Don't misspell it DIMOND.

FIERY—don't make a mistake and write FIRE–Y, it's FIER–Y.

GAUGE—don't misspell it GAGE. This is the only word in which AU is pronounced as a long A.

LEOPARD—EO is pronounced as a short E. Don't misspell it LEPARD.

PEOPLE—EO is pronounced as a long E. Don't misspell it PEEPLE.

SERGEANT—the ER is pronounced as if it is AR. The last half of the word is tricky too. Don't misspell it SARGENT.

Aa Bb Cc Dd Ee Ff Gg Hh Ii

SOPHOMORE—means a 10th grader, or someone in her second year at college. Don't forget that it has three Os. A lot of people tend to forget the O after SOPH. Don't misspell it SOPHMORE.

SUCCEED—remember those two Cs. Don't misspell it SUCEED.

VACUUM—one C, two Us. Don't misspell it VACUME.

WOMAN/WOMEN—try to remember that WOMAN contains the word MAN. WOMEN is the plural; it contains the word MEN.

Aa Bb Cc Dd Ee Ff Gg Hh Ii Jj

Find and correct the errors. The number of errors is placed in parentheses after the sentence.

1. The whole inside of our house turned into a firey inferno! (1)

2. I'm too bizzy to sing in the quire. (2)

3. The gage's needle is in the red zone! It's going to blow up! (1)

4. The lepard licked his chops and looked thoughtfully at Sargent Chang. (2)

5. Will you peeple shut up?! (1)

6. I want all the wimen to sing the first verse, and all the men to sing the second. (1)

7. Is she a sophmore or a junior? (1)

8. Look at that women with the green hair and the nose ring. (1)

9. Did you get a look at the dimond he gave her? (1)

10. If you want to suceed on the baseball dimund, you have to practice—and then practice some more. (2)

Aa Bb Cc Dd Ee Ff Gg Hh Ii Jj

11. Outer space is a total vacume. (1)

12. You're going to think I'm crazy, but that leperd just turned into a women! (1)

13. I'll tell you what he's got between his ears—pure vacume! (1)

14. The wimin got so mad, their faces turned firey red. (2)

15. All you peeple who want to sign up for kwire, raise your hands.(2)

16. The lepard was so bizzy chasing the antelope that he didn't notice the hunter hiding in the tree. (2)

17. The way I gage peeple is by how nice they are to their mothers. (2)

18. When the police sargent booked the thief, he found two rubies, three opals, and a dimond in his pockets. (2)

19. To suceed in making a vacume, watch the gage on this pump. (3)

20. The womin came straight up to the leperd and slapped him on the nose. She looked right into his firey eyes and laughed. All the other wimin gasped. (4)

see page 252 for answers

Chapter 12:
Like Cats and Dogs

Spelling contests are fun activities and a good way to quiz yourself and your friends.

If Beauregard had realized that the giant dog Woof was standing in the doorway right behind him, he would probably have shut up. It is hard to say for sure. There are a few cats in this world who can tolerate the company of dogs. There are even a few cats who actually like dogs. Beauregard was not one of them. He did not like dogs. He thought it would be a good idea to put all the dogs in the world in a space ship and send them straight to the moon.

"To say the least," said Beauregard, "dogs are stupid. They look dumb, and they are dumb. Take my word for it. The average barnyard fowl is fifty IQ points brighter than the smartest of dogs. The idea that a dog can spell—ha! You might as well say a dog can do calculus. Dogs can't speak. They can't understand any words. Well—sit. 'Sit' is one of the few words a dog can understand."

Behind Beauregard, Woof sat down.

Biff pointed at Woof and laughed.

"And 'play dead,'" Beauregard said.

"Play dead!" Biff commanded.

The giant dog slumped to his side and closed his eyes. He opened his mouth slightly and let his long, pink tongue hang out.

Bridget laughed so hard she had to cover her mouth.

When Beauregard spun around to see what Biff and Bridget were laughing at, he saw the biggest dog he had ever seen in his life. Even lying down for all intents and purposes dead, Woof was a startling sight to behold. He was about the size of a cow.

"Hey, Woof," Biff said, "wake up and say hello to Beauregard. You guys are gonna have a spelling contest!"

The enormous dog jumped to his feet. To Beauregard, the dog seemed only slightly smaller than an elephant.

Woof cocked his head and looked thoughtfully at the cat as a very hungry person might look at plate of dessert.

"Yikes!" Beauregard said. He tried to look as big and dangerous as possible. He arched his back. His hair stood on end. But no matter what the cat did, he seemed tiny compared to the dog. Look for cover, he thought. Maybe I can hide under the bed.

Woof lifted an ear. He had never before met a talking cat, and seemed fascinated to meet one now. "Yip," Woof said. It was his idea of a friendly bark, but the sound was so loud, it scared Beauregard half to death. He leapt straight into Barnaby's arms.

"Hey!" Barnaby yelled.

"Don't worry," Biff said. "Woof won't hurt you." He walked up to the giant beast, reached up, and scratched him under the chin. "You're a friendly old dog, aren't you, Woof?"

Beauregard leapt down onto the floor again. "Who's scared? I'm not at all scared!"

"Yup," said Woof. His tail thumped the floor so hard that a book fell out of the bookcase.

"Are we supposed to believe that this…this moose can spell? Ridiculous." He quickly hid behind Barnaby.

"Woof!" barked Woof. His tail thumped the floor again and two more books crashed to the floor.

"Watch this!" Biff said. The good-looking kid ran to his closet and brought out a big bag of magnetic letters, the kind that can stick to refrigerators to make words. "Woof's no good at writing. He can't manage the piece of chalk with his mouth. The King and the Queen figured this out. They're really great at teaching. According to them, almost anyone can learn anything if you figure out a good way to teach them." Biff dumped the letters out onto the floor. He went back into his closet and came out with a metal board. "What should we have him spell?"

"Why not something terribly difficult?" Beauregard said sarcastically. "CAT."

"OK, Woof," Biff said, "spell CAT."

To the amazement of Beauregard, Bridget, and Barnaby, the giant dog walked over to the letters and peered down at them. Then he leaned down, picked up a letter with his mouth, and dropped it onto the metal board. He found a second letter, dropped it, then found a third letter. With a giant paw, Woof arranged the three letters. He admired his handiwork for a moment, then stepped back from the board and sat down.

The kids ran forward to look. There on the board were the letters K–A–T.

"Ha!" Beauregard said. "What a genius." He figured it was going to be easy to clobber this big stupid dog in a spelling contest.

"Hey, Beauregard, why don't you spell DOG?" Biff said. "Woof, you sit over there in the corner so you won't make Beauregard nervous."

The big dog obediently went to the corner and sat down. "Woof."

Beauregard poked around the letters, dropped one on the metal board. He tossed down two more. Then, to everyone's surprise, Beauregard selected a fourth letter from the pile and dropped it on the board. He moved the letters around with his right paw, then stood back. "Now, give me something hard!" he said scornfully.

The kids crowded around.

On the board were the letters D–A–W–G.

Bridget put her hand over her mouth. She winked at Barnaby. "I won't laugh if you won't!"

"No kidding." Barnaby rubbed his bushy red hair and grinned.

There was a knock on the door. "Come in!" Biff yelled. "It's not locked!"

The door swung open; it was the King. Right beside him was the Guard of Spelling. The Guard was still dressed up in his suit of armor. He had a sort of pie plate on his head. The two ends of his mustache struck straight out like two paint brushes.

His Majesty smiled at everyone. "Oh good, Woof, you're already here! And you've met the talking cat!" He turned back to the Guard and motioned him into the room. "Come on in, Sir Pete. You're going to be the judge!"

The Guard twirled his mustache and sniffed haughtily.

The King explained how the contest was going to work. First, Bridget and Barnaby would coach Beauregard. At the same time, Biff and the King would coach Woof. They would use some commonly misspelled words, plus a similar-size list that the Guard would provide. "Have you got it ready, Sir Pete?"

The Guard drew out a long piece of paper. He had circled several words—hard ones.

"Go on," the King said, "read them out to us!"

"ACTUALLY," the Guard said. He cleared his throat. "AT-TEMPTS, CUPBOARD," Sir Pete momentarily lowered his list and grinned at the King. "I especially love that one!"

"It's a tough one all right!" the King agreed.

The Guard continued, "ENVIRONMENT, GOVERNMENT."

"Wow," Bridget said, "this is gonna be some contest."

Sir Pete held up his hand. "No interruptions, please." He looked sternly at Bridget.

"Sorry," Bridget mumbled.

"PLAID, RASPBERRY, RECOGNIZE, SEVERAL."

Barnaby groaned. This really was a hard list. He wasn't at all sure he knew how to spell some of these words. He wondered if RASPBERRY might be spelled RAZZBERRY. "I have to find a dictionary," he thought.

"SURPRISE, TEMPERATURE, and...," the Guard lowered the list. He twirled his mustache, "last, but not least—YACHT!"

Beauregard's tail drooped to the ground. His shoulders slumped. Who could spell such hard words? What had he gotten himself into! He looked over at Woof.

The dog had tilted his big head toward the door and one ear was cocked. The dog didn't seem to be paying the slightest attention to Sir Pete and his spelling list. What was it? Did Woof hear something?

There was a gentle knock at the door.

The King smiled. "I'd know that knock anywhere. Come in, darling!"

Her Majesty's voice rang out, "Is Beauregard in there, dear?"

"He sure is!"

"We've got a surprise for him!"

Barnaby heard a couple of stifled giggles that sounded as if they might be coming from Beth and Babette.

The door slowly swung open.

Beauregard ran forward; he waved his tail with excitement and yelled, "Cleopatra! Is it you?"

Cleopatra walked into the room. She was an absolutely gorgeous fluffy white cat with a red ribbon tied around her neck.

"We met Cleopatra outside," the Queen said. "She's come to see the contest. I think she and Beauregard are old friends."

Cleopatra looked at Beauregard. She sat down on the floor and purred loudly, then licked one of her paws.

Beauregard had been thinking about dropping out of the contest. Who wanted to learn all those hard words anyway? But now that Cleopatra was here, he was eager to win and impress her. He'd smash that big dog to pieces and show Cleopatra what a smart cat he was!

Beauregard sat down beside the beautiful white cat. He leaned over and licked her cheek. "Cleo, honey, you are just about the best-looking kitty cat in the whole wide world, you know that? Hang around awhile and watch me make a monkey out of this dog."

Cleopatra purred contently. She really was a splendid cat. And she didn't like dogs any better than Beauregard did.

Biff said, "Who knew a cool-looking cat like Cleopatra would go for a bad speller?"

"Hey," Bridget said, "you guys hear that?"

"Yeah," Barnaby looked toward the window, "what is it?"

"Sounded like a bark," Biff said. He ran over to look out of the window.

"Oh, no," Babette said, "that's not a bark. Listen—it's a meow."

Bridget ran to the window. She stood beside Barnaby and peered down into the street. "Oh man, this is unbelievable!" Bridget turned to the others. "You guys better come look at this!"

Everyone crowded around the window. On the sidewalk in front of the Palace stood a calico cat. Not far away stood a Boston terrier.

"Meow," said the calico.

"Arf," said the terrier.

"They want to come see the spelling contest!" Biff yelled.

An Afghan hound walked around the corner and sat down beside the terrier. A gray Persian came from the other direction and sat down beside the calico cat. A Boxer ran around the corner, then a Chihuahua and a Bulldog. From the other direction came a short-haired black cat, a fluffy blond cat, and two little black and white kittens.

"I can't believe this," Beth whispered. "Word's got out."

"It's every cat and dog in the neighborhood!" yelled Biff. "They've all come to see the contest!"

From every direction, cats and dogs arrived, until there were so many animals standing on the sidewalk, it was impossible to walk past them.

Beauregard fluffed himself up and stood on his hind legs. "Come on, Cleopatra." He started toward the door. "We'd better find an auditorium! It's just like I said. The honor of all cats is at stake with this contest! And there's nothing I like better than a big audience!"

Woof stood to his feet. He ambled over to the window and looked down at all the pets in the street. "Yup!" he barked.

Exercises for Chapter 12

On one side of the auditorium stage, the King and Biff coached Woof; on the other, Bridget and Barnaby coached Beauregard. They worked on learning to spell all the words listed in the back of the last chapter, as well as the new ones the Guard had given them when they were in Biff's room. Sir Pete had a very long list of words that are hard to spell. He called them his Word Hoard and was especially fond of the words that were hardest to spell.

Since all the other dogs and cats were filing into the Palace auditorium, the coaches didn't have much time. They had to work fast!

A Dozen Hard-to-Spell Words from Sir Pete's Word Hoard

ACTUALLY—remember that ACTUALLY starts with the word ACT. Don't misspell it ACUALLY or AXUALLY.

ATTEMPTS—it's easy to forget that final T. Don't misspell it ATTEMPS.

CUPBOARD—this word is spelled CUP + BOARD. It helps to visualize a big board with a hook from which hangs a cup. Don't misspell it CUBBORD.

Aa Bb Cc Dd Ee Ff Gg Hh Ii Jj

ENVIRONMENT—it may help to remember that in the middle of ENV*IRON*MENT is the word IRON. Don't misspell it ENVIORMENT or ENVIRORNMENT.

GOVERNMENT—Think of this word as GOVERN + MENT so you won't forget the N in the middle. Don't misspell it GOVERMENT.

PLAID—AI is pronounced like a short A; don't misspell it PLAD. It may help to remember that the word PL*AID* ends with the word AID; think of someone wearing PLAID coming to your AID.

RASPBERRY—although it sounds like RAZZBERRY, don't forget that silent P.

RECOGNIZE—don't forget that G in the middle. Don't misspell it RECONIZE.

SEVERAL—it is easy to forget the E in the middle. Don't misspell it SEVRAL.

SURPRISE—remember that SURPRISE has two Rs and no Z. It is easy to leave out the first R. Don't misspell it SUPRISE or SURPRIZE.

TEMPERATURE—don't forget that A; it is easy to misspell this word TEMPERTURE.

YACHT—watch out for that silent C in the middle. Don't misspell it YAT or YAHT.

Find and correct the mistakes in the following sentences. The number of mistakes is in parentheses.

1. Axually, the thief made five attemps to break into the secret room. (2)

2. The goverment agent kept all the secret codes locked up in a hidden cubbord. (2)

3. Our teacher really cares about the enviroment; she says we all have to recycle. (1)

4. Which do you like better, this razzberry vest or this plad one? (2)

5. Akually, she didn't even reconize us. (2)

6. Sevral of us hid in the big cubberd. When Max opened the door, boy, was he suprized! (3)

7. The day we went out on the duke's yaht, the temperture was nearly freezing. (2)

8. I think the goverment needs to do something about the enviornment. (2)

9. Did you take Kelly's temperture? I'd be suprised if she doesn't have a fever. (2)

Aa Bb Cc Dd Ee Ff Gg Hh Ii Jj

10. Did you rekognize that new ice cream was razberry ripple? (2)

11. I was really surprised to see that the winning yat's main sail was plad. Maybe somebody from Scotland owns it. (3)

12. After sevral attemps, the cow jumped over the moon. The spoon and the dish were so surprized, they ran away together. (3)

13. I stayed on that diet for two weeks. Big suprize—I acually gained weight! (2)

14. After sevral more attemps, Meagan finally succeeded in measuring the temperture of the mud at the bottom of the lake. (3)

15. I heard the goverment seized that yaht because the owner was involved in illegal activities! (2)

16. We keep all the razzberry syrup in the yellow cupbord. (2)

17. In that high-crime enviorment, it's a suprize that Joe gets such good grades. (2)

18. Do you reconize her? She's the one who's attemping to walk to the North Pole! (2)

see page 253 for answers

Have a spelling contest with your friends using the list from Sir Pete's Word Hoard.

Chapter 13:
Tail Feathers

Can you spell all the months of the year? What about the second month, which is really hard to spell?

The Duchess owned a parrot, a perfectly splendid bird with long green tail feathers. The Guard owned a pet monkey that he kept in his quarters. At least he *tried* to keep the monkey in his quarters. Although in most ways a friendly and sensible animal, the monkey possessed one bad habit: curiosity. That monkey could not help himself. He had to see everything. No matter how much trouble the Guard went to make the monkey stay in his room, the monkey would manage to sneak out and explore. The monkey was especially fond of snooping in the rooms of the Palace where he was forbidden to enter. Of all the forbidden places, his favorite room to sneak into was that of the Duchess. Her room contained something the monkey wanted badly: tail feathers from her parrot.

The Duchess would leave her room and would forget to close the window or neglect to lock the door. The monkey would sneak in, and a minute later, the parrot would let out a blood-curdling shriek. The Duchess would run back to her room. She'd throw open the door, and there would be her parrot, minus another of his long, green tail feathers.

No one was absolutely sure where the monkey kept his collection of tail feathers, but everyone in the Palace was certain he definitely had a collection. According to Biff and Beth, sometimes they would wake up in the middle of the night and look out the window and catch a glimpse of something that looked a lot like the monkey running along the roof, waving and flapping the tail feathers as if he were trying to fly.

The day of the big spelling contest, there were so many dogs and cats in the auditorium that the place was on the verge of chaos. That is when the parrot flew in the open doorway at the back of the auditorium. He sailed in a big, lazy semicircle over the heads of the dogs and cats. The dogs and cats looked up and saw the green sailing bird and went totally bananas. Cats leapt, dogs jumped. In a moment, the air was full of the writhing bodies of the animals that were trying to grab the parrot. Naturally, the fact that dozens of huge dogs and ferocious cats were trying to grab him caused the parrot a few moments of uneasiness, to say the least. He looked wildly around the room and finally spotted the Duchess on the stage whispering into the ear of the Queen and dove at her. Very likely, the parrot meant to land on the Duchess's shoulder, but it miscalculated somehow. Perhaps because he was missing so many of his tail feathers, his flying ability was not what it once was. The parrot missed her shoulder and collided with the curtain at the rear of the stage.

"Oh, dear," the Duchess cried, "Sweetums, are you all right?" Yes, the parrot did have the unfortunate name Sweetums. The Duchess scooped up her pet and looked at it carefully to see if he was all right.

At that moment, the monkey strolled into the back of the auditorium. He stood up on its hind legs, observed the commotion on the stage where the Duchess was examining her parrot, then leapt onto the neck of a Labrador retriever and rode that animal bareback to the front of the auditorium, where the monkey dismounted and leapt up onto the stage.

The Guard saw his pet scrambling over the lip of the stage and realized at once that the Duchess (she was cradling Sweetums and cooing to him) would not be happy if she knew the monkey was nearby. The Duchess did not like the monkey. She did not approve of him. "Monkeys," she was fond of saying, "are dirty. They are thieves. They do not belong in a Palace. They belong in zoos!" The Duchess especially resented the fact that the monkey stole her parrot's tail feathers. Poor Sweetums had been robbed so often that he now possessed only two of the long, gracefully curved feathers.

Hoping to avoid an argument, the Guard grabbed his pet monkey and stuck him inside his breastplate. The Guard's armor did not fit very well. It had been made for a man a good deal thicker in the chest than the Guard, so there was plenty of room inside it for a monkey to curl up and go to sleep. Once inside the breastplate, the monkey quieted down, but he certainly did not fall asleep. If anyone had looked closely at the Guard, he might have noticed the monkey's bright eyes peering out of the breastplate. Fortunately, or perhaps unfortunately, there was so much else to look at in the auditorium that no one looked closely.

The Queen raised her hands. She walked to the front of the stage. "Hello, everyone! Welcome to the Palace of Words! How nice of you to come!"

If someone had strode to the edge of the stage and yelled at all the dogs and cats to shut up, it is likely that not a single one of them would have paid the slightest attention. But the tall queen was so friendly, she was so gracious and hospitable, so dignified, yet kindly, that she hardly had to say two words before every single dog and cat in the room shut up and sat in its chair looking at her as thoughtfully as if it hoped she might soon throw out handfuls of delicious dog biscuits and catnip.

The Queen announced, "As you all know, our original plan was to have a contest between Beauregard, the most intelligent cat in the world and Woof, the best speller in the history of dogkind. But the King and I have second thoughts. Biff here, has been working day and night on his spelling. This kid here, Bridget, is one of the best spellers her age in all the state of New York; her friends Barnaby and Babette are pretty good spellers, and of course Beth—the writer of mystery stories—is excellent. Well, why not let them all participate? If you all approve, the King and I will conduct a spelling bee!"

Dogs barked, cats yowled showing their enthusiasm about the chance to see so many contestants. While the audience was yelping and howling, Biff ran up to the Queen and whispered in her ear.

"Do you think we should?" she laughed and motioned to the King. "Pop, come here." The Queen whispered into the King's ear. He smiled and nodded.

The Queen raised her hands again and the animals quieted down at once. "Biff has suggested that the King and I participate. In fact, he's challenged us. What do you think? Should we join the spelling bee?"

The animals noisily signaled their agreement.

"Then we will!"

"Yoohoo!" The Duchess extracted the hanky from her sleeve and waved it in the air. The parrot was now perched on her shoulder. It cocked its head to one side and examined the waving hanky as if it would like to eat it. "Your Majesty, I would like to participate too, if I may!"

"Why, of course you can, Ruthie," the Queen said.

"The more the merrier," Bridget agreed.

The Guard announced he had added to the list of words, "I've pulled out some extra hard words from my Word Hoard!" He unfolded his long list and waved it in the air and then peered at it, twirling the end of his mustache with one hand.

"Now, don't be too hard on us, dear!" the Duchess cried.

The Guard lowered the list and glared at the Duchess until she blushed and looked down at her feet. He seemed to take his official duties as judge very seriously.

"I've picked out another dozen words—excruciatingly difficult ones!" The Guard smiled grimly. The very idea that anyone would suggest he should come up with easy ones seemed to irritate him.

The Duchess made a little shiver with her shoulders, which caused the parrot to flap its wings and squawk. While everyone was looking at the parrot, the monkey leapt out of the Guard's breastplate and ran behind the curtain at the back of the stage. No one noticed him. The monkey lifted the bottom of the curtain and peeked out. He seemed especially interested in the parrot and its two wonderfully green tail feathers.

The contest began. The Guard lined up the contestants in front of the curtain. Chairs were set up at stage left for the contestants who lost. The audience listened carefully as the Guard pronounced the first word to the first contestant. "Biff, your word is FEBRUARY."

Biff took a deep breath and closed his eyes. What was it about FEBRUARY? He remembered there was something weird about the word—a silent R. His eyes popped open, "F–E–B–R," he said the R especially loudly, "U–A–R–Y! FEBRUARY."

"Correct!" said the Guard.

"Whew," Biff whispered.

All but one of the contestants survived the first round. Babette got the word LABORATORY and remembered that it starts with the word LABOR. The King got the word CHOIR. He tickled his chin for a second, thought of the CHOIR singing a CHOrd, and then spelled it quickly. Woof's first word was LEOPARD. It took the big dog awhile to drop the letters onto the metal board and arrange them with his paws, but when he was done, the Guard held up the board, and there was the word LEOPARD spelled perfectly. All the dogs in the audience barked enthusiastically, but several of the cats hissed loudly. The Duchess tapped one cheek with an index finger, then spelled SERGEANT. Beauregard waved his tail several times, then successfully spelled PLAID. All the cats in the audience settled down into their seats and purred. The Queen spelled DIAMOND. Bridget had no trouble spelling SEVERAL.

The only one to go out the first round was Barnaby. He got the tricky word FOREIGN, and he misspelled it FOREIN. The Guard made him sit down on one of the chairs at the side of the stage.

The second round did not go so smoothly. Biff got the word ATHLETE. He closed his eyes again. What was weird about the word? He opened his eyes and spelled it ATHALETE.

"Wrong! Biff's out!" yelled the Guard. He twirled his mustache. "There's no A in the middle, son. It's ATHLETE."

"That's okay Biff," Barnaby said when Biff sat down on the chair beside his. "That was a tough one."

Babette stumbled over the word CUPBOARD, forgetting the CUP + BOARD hint. She misspelled it CUBBERD and had to sit down.

The King got the word FIERY. He frowned and asked, "Could I hear it used in a sentence?" He took off his crown and held it in his fists.

The Guard felt about inside his breastplate and realized he was missing something. He looked up into the ceiling of auditorium, above the stage where all the lamps and wires were hung. "FIERY. His angry face was red and FIERY." The Guard looked at his watch. "You have one minute, your Majesty." He gazed into the wings at the right side of the stage.

"Let me see; let me see," the King twisted his crown around in a circle, then popped it back onto his head. "F–E–I–R–Y!" He looked hopefully at the Guard.

"Wrong!" yelled Sir Pete. "It's *I* before *E*, sir. You will have to take a seat." The Guard pointed to the chairs, where Barnaby, Biff, and Babette already sat.

The curtain directly behind the Duchess made a little jerk as if it had been touched by a small breeze. Woof's second word was RASPBERRY. The dog dropped several letters onto the metal board, then stared at the result for a long time and finally added one more letter. He pushed it into position with his paw and then said, "Woof!"

The Guard held up the board and shouted, "Correct!" He looked down at Woof. "You had a little trouble with that silent P, didn't you?"

"Yup," the big dog barked. All the dogs in the audience yipped and yapped to show their enthusiasm for Woof. The cats looked the other way and yawned.

The Duchess had no trouble with the word SOPHOMORE. She remembered SOPHOMORE has three Os and loudly pronounced the second one, the one easiest to forget. Beauregard got a tricky word—LOSE. "Could you use it in a sentence?" His furry ears twitched.

The Guard sniffed. He seemed a little distracted and was looking around the stage. "Be careful when you go to bat, or else we will LOSE the game. You have one minute."

Beauregard remembered that it is easy to get confused about LOSE and LOOSE. LOOSE rhymes with GOOSE, he remembered. Thank goodness Bridget had taught him that little saying. So LOSE must be the one that had only one O. "L–O–S–E? Lose?" he asked.

The Guard yelled, "Correct!" The cats in the audience purred loudly. The curtain behind the Duchess bulged a little as if something behind it was edging forward.

The Queen spelled VACUUM. She remembered that the word has two Us but had to think a moment before she was sure that it had only one C.

Bridget spelled YACHT. With that silent C in the middle it is a tricky word, but she had no trouble with it. She wasn't the champion speller of her school by accident.

"Round Three!" the Guard yelled. "No more easy words!"

"Easy?" Bridget muttered. "What does he mean, easy? He hasn't given an easy word yet!"

The King jumped to his feet and held up his arms, "Time for a stretch break!"

All the remaining contestants, Woof, the Duchess, Beauregard, the Queen, and Bridget, bent and stretched their arms and legs. In the audience, the dogs and cats also took the opportunity to stretch. No one was looking at the curtain at the rear of the stage, but if anyone had been looking, they might have noticed a tiny, black paw holding up its edge.

The Guard glared at his watch. He seemed impatient to get to the end of the contest. He swiveled his head from side to side and peered into the wings at either side of the stage. The parrot clutched the Duchess's shoulder tightly and stretched out his left wing, then his right. He then fluffed up his long, green, tail feathers, then made them lay flat. The Duchess took her place back by the curtain.

"Okay," Bridget said. "Let's go. We're ready!"

"Woof," the Guard said, "your word is—GUARANTEE."

The giant dog stood up and looked down at the pile of letters at his feet. He began to pick up letters and toss them onto the metal board. When he was done, he moved them here and there with his paw. He looked at the letters, cocked his head, and moved the letters again.

"Woof's in trouble," Biff whispered to Barnaby. "GUARAN-TEE—that's a super hard word!"

"Time's up!" the Guard yelled. He bent down and picked up the board. Everyone leaned forward to see what was written on it. Unfortunately, before the Guard could turn around and swing the board out into the light where everyone could see it, something happened, something rather complicated, something that caused the spelling bee to come to an abrupt conclusion.

The parrot screamed. The word *scream* hardly seems sufficient to describe the hair-raising, terrifying, ear-splitting cry of rage and humiliation that came from Sweetums. The bird leapt into the air. He leapt so quickly that it seemed as if he had been fired out of a cannon.

The parrot flew. Unfortunately, Sweetums did not fly in a straight line. Something was wrong with the bird. He was completely without tail feathers! If not altogether dependent on his tail feathers to fly, the bird was used to them. He depended on those two feathers for balance. Without his tail feathers, Sweetums seemed almost drunk.

The bird spun off-balance into a curtain. He tried to regain his perch on the Duchess's shoulder but missed. His left talon seized her hair. The bird flapped wildly and flew away carrying...was it a cat?

The Duchess screamed.

If the scream emitted by the parrot when he lost his very last two tail feathers was hair-raising, the scream emitted by the Duchess when her wig was torn from her head was so loud, so piercing and ear-splitting, that it seemed as if a siren had gone off.

Still carrying the wig, the crazed parrot flew out over the audience. It dropped the hairpiece onto the head of a German shepherd. At the sight of the green bird careening just over their heads, the dogs and cats went into an insane frenzy. They tried to catch Sweetums. Several dogs, animals with amazing springs in their back legs, leapt six feet in the air. So many cats dived down from the balcony that it almost seemed to be raining cats.

Sweetums flew wildly about the auditorium. Frightened out of his wits, he spotted a rectangle of light at the very back of the auditorium, which appeared to be an open window. Desperately, the bird flapped until it gained enough altitude to swoop from the front to the back of the auditorium. He flew right out a door, crossed the lobby, and disappeared into the men's restroom. Earlier in the day, a janitor had been cleaning the restroom and had propped open the door with a bucket.

There was a rather sickening thump.

Silence descended.

"You've killed him! You've killed Sweetums!" the Duchess yelled. With her hands over her nearly bald head, she ran down the aisle to the restroom.

There, in a sink, on his back, his golden talons sticking up, was Sweetums. The parrot had mistakenly thought the rectangle of light was an open window and had flown directly into it. Unfortunately it was actually a mirror.

The Duchess scooped up the parrot. She held Sweetums cradled in her arms as if he were a baby and ran weeping out of the restroom and down the hallway toward her room. She stopped, turned on her heel, and returned to the auditorium. Neither the people on stage nor the dogs and cats uttered a single sound. The Guard stood in the middle of the stage. He had a funny expression on his face and looked as if someone had just hit him over the head with a bat. He was still holding the metal board on which was written GARENTEE.

"Your monkey!" the Duchess screamed. "You! You! Tail feathers! Killers! Murderers! All of you!" She clutched Sweetums to her chest and ran down the hallway.

Aa Bb Cc Dd Ee Ff Gg Hh Ii Jj
Kk Ll Mm Nn Oo Pp Qq Rr Ss Tt Uu Vv Ww Xx Yy Zz

Exercises for Chapter 13

These are the extra hard words the Guard picked out for the contest. They aren't easy to learn!

ATHLETE—Biff found out what makes this word tricky. It does not contain an E or an A in the middle. Spell it ATHLETE.

CONVENIENT—the first two syllables are pretty easy. This is one of those tricky IENT words. Don't misspell it CONVENYUNT.

FOREIGN—this is the word that tripped up Barnaby. It may help to remember that it contains the word REIGN (The foreign king's REIGN lasted for twenty years).

GUARANTEE—this word was too much for Woof. Two As and two Es. Don't misspell it GARENTEE.

IMMEDIATELY—if you remember that there are two Ms, and you sound this word out slowly, you should be able to spell it. Don't forget the E before the LY. IMMEDIATE-LY.

JUDGMENT—don't put an E at the end of the first syllable.

LICENSE—the C and S make this one tricky. Don't misspell it LICENCE.

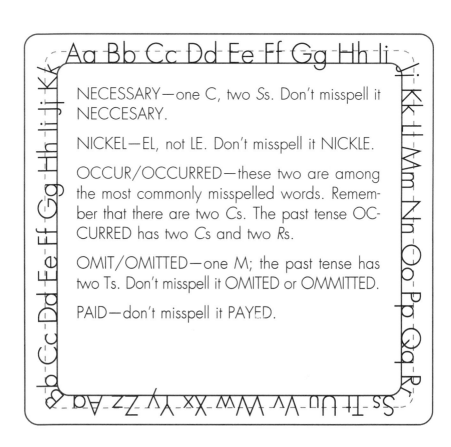

Aa Bb Cc Dd Ee Ff Gg Hh Ii

NECESSARY—one C, two Ss. Don't misspell it NECCESARY.

NICKEL—EL, not LE. Don't misspell it NICKLE.

OCCUR/OCCURRED—these two are among the most commonly misspelled words. Remember that there are two Cs. The past tense OCCURRED has two Cs and two Rs.

OMIT/OMITTED—one M; the past tense has two Ts. Don't misspell it OMITED or OMMITTED.

PAID—don't misspell it PAYED.

Aa Bb Cc Dd Ee Ff Gg Hh Ii Jj

Find and correct the mistakes in the following sentences. The number of mistakes is in parentheses at the end of the sentences.

1. He's an athelete? Big deal! He should still do his homework! (1)

2. I guarentee, if you pay attention to what Mrs. Chong says, you'll get your driving licence. (2)

3. In our judgement, you should catch the boa constrictor imediately! (2)

4. Sure, we can do it, lady, but it's not convenyunt. (1)

5. I can't believe this candy only costs a nickle! (1)

6. When the robbery ocurred, I garentee none of my kids were nearby. (2)

7. In my jugement, we payed way too much for that. (2)

8. Antonio's the best athalete on the team. (1)

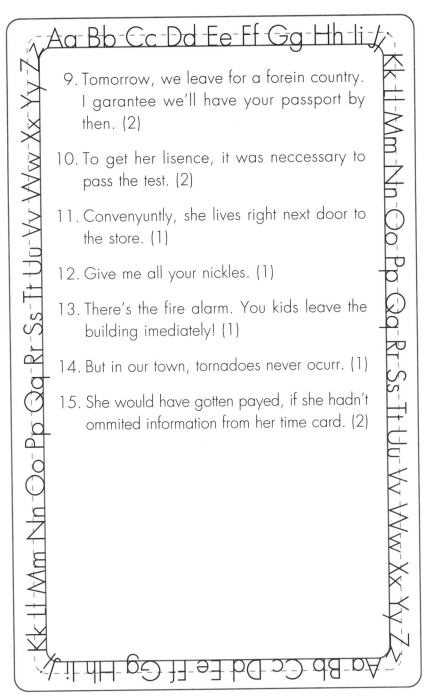

9. Tomorrow, we leave for a forein country. I garantee we'll have your passport by then. (2)

10. To get her lisence, it was neccessary to pass the test. (2)

11. Convenyuntly, she lives right next door to the store. (1)

12. Give me all your nickles. (1)

13. There's the fire alarm. You kids leave the building imediately! (1)

14. But in our town, tornadoes never ocurr. (1)

15. She would have gotten payed, if she hadn't ommited information from her time card. (2)

see page 253 for answers

In the last four chapters, you've learned more than fifty new words—and lots of tricky ones. Let's try a review test. If you miss some, don't freak out. You are learning many of the most commonly misspelled words in the English language. If you find a lot of the mistakes in the following sentences, that is really great! If you get them ALL right, wow, you are a champion speller! Reward yourself. Get some exercise. Do something really fun! If you miss quite a few, don't get depressed. Lots of people make mistakes with these words. You are learning to spell more and more words, and that's what is important. Even the Guard of Spelling would probably miss some of these words!

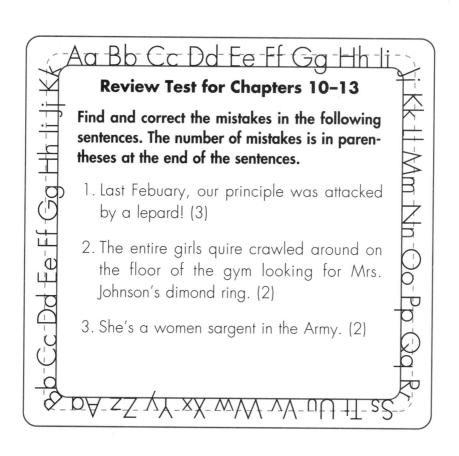

Review Test for Chapters 10–13

Find and correct the mistakes in the following sentences. The number of mistakes is in parentheses at the end of the sentences.

1. Last Febuary, our principle was attacked by a lepard! (3)

2. The entire girls quire crawled around on the floor of the gym looking for Mrs. Johnson's dimond ring. (2)

3. She's a women sargent in the Army. (2)

4. Inside the firey furnace, the temperture was over one thousand degrees. (2)

5. According to that gage, we have achieved an almost perfect vacume. (2)

6. Four the forth time, you peeple are not supposed to talk when the teacher's talking! (3)

7. They garentee their yahts will never develop engine trouble. (2)

8. To suceed, the athelete had to make many atemps. (3)

9. She wore a plad skirt and a razberry hat. (2)

10. After they turned their workroom into a labratory, I couldn't even rekonize the place. (2)

11. All those young wimen are sophmores. (2)

12. Sevral forein spies were discovered hiding in the big cubberd. (3)

13. In my jeweler's judgement, all fourty of those dimens have flaws. (3)

14. Sevral of our athaletes ommitted the answer from the test. (3)

15. The main affect of all this rain on our envirunment is mudslides. (2)

16. She payed way too much four that computer. It's not even garenteed. (3)

17. I want you peeple to leave imediatly. (2)

18. I don't care if it is convenyunt to lie, it's the principal of the thing! (2)

19. Amy didn't get her lisence; she actualy ran a red light while taking her driving test! (2)

20. When the earthquake ocured, Mr. Robinson was standing directly on top of the fault line. Boy, was he suprized! (2)

see page 254 for answers

Chapter 14:
His Majesty
Gets Angry

If you ever want
to get married,
you need to
learn how to
spell it:
MARRIAGE!

The Queen and the Duchess Ruthie were in the Duchess's room, sitting on her bed. The Duchess waved her handkerchief in the air as if it were a little white flag. Then she crumpled it up into a ball and used it to pat her cheeks. They were bright red. Her eyes were wet and swollen. Her glasses were smeared. They'd slid quite a long way down her nose, so far that periodically the Duchess had to shove them back up with her finger or else they'd have dropped to the floor. Ruthie wasn't wearing her wig, and without it, her head was not really bald, but you could see her pink scalp gleaming through the thin hair.

The Duchess wailed, "Remember what the only word he's ever misspelled is? MARRIAGE! He spelled it M–A–R–R–A–G–E." She shoved up her glasses. "I should have known then—the Guard of Spelling couldn't spell MARRIAGE!"

The Queen patted her on the shoulder. "Oh, for heaven's sake, Ruthie, everyone misspells a few words. I don't think it means anything." She handed Ruthie a tissue.

"He spells every word in the universe right, but not MARRIAGE! If that isn't a clue, I don't know what is! He will never marry me—never, never, never!"

The Queen put her arm around her sister-in-law's shoulders and squeezed. "Now, now, Ruthie, not everyone has to get married. Lots of people never do."

"I will bury Sweetums; I will bury the poor dear in the garden." The Duchess blew loudly into the tissue. "I've put him in my sewing box." The Duchess pointed to a very beautiful sewing box on a nearby table. "Hand painted."

The Queen nodded; no doubt that explained the spools of thread that were unrolling on the floor.

"Don't you think it is a perfectly beautiful box? My embroidery box."

"Yes, Ruthie."

"An appropriate box . . . for a coffin?"

"It is one of the most splendid coffins I have ever seen," her Majesty assured Ruthie. "Especially for a parrot."

"I wrapped him in black silk. Oh, my poor, poor Sweetums!" The Duchess flung the Kleenex over her face and sobbed loudly into it.

The Queen kissed her cheek.

"I will bury Sweetums in the garden, then depart the Palace forever, sadder and wiser. Some are born never to find mates, to walk the world alone—tragic figures. I am one of those, your Majesty."

"Oh, Ruthie, for heaven's sake, you don't need to leave us!"

"I have made an irrevocable decision. I will leave the Palace forever. I have spent entirely too much time hanging around waiting for that man to recover his wits. I can't bear to stay here another moment. He's a madman, a monster in human form, who trained his monkey to attack and finally murder my parrot! Poor, poor Sweetums!"

"Surely Pete did not train the monkey to do any such thing. I am sure Sir Pete is just as sorry as anyone about what happened."

"I will retreat to a nunnery and lock myself up forever."

"But you aren't Catholic, dear."

"Well, if I can't do that. . . I. . . I will join the French Foreign Legion."

"But I don't think they take women, do they? And besides, you aren't even French."

"I will join the International Red Cross—I will travel the world—from natural disaster to natural disaster until I find peace and forgetfulness—perhaps a leper colony somewhere needs a helping hand."

"A leper colony! You can't be serious?"

"Perhaps in Bolivia or New Zealand. Do you think they still have lepers in New Zealand?"

"It's a modern country, Ruthie, I am sure they have excellent medical facilities. I don't think. . . "

"One day, we will look back on this and laugh, don't you think?" The Duchess tried to smile but only burst into more sobs.

The Queen looked at her doubtfully. "Ruthie, you need to calm down. Rest, try to sleep."

"I don't care about him, not one bit." The Duchess took off her glasses and dabbed her eyes. "I am completely over him. I mean it. When I bury Sweetums in the garden, I will also bury our love. The greatest passion of my life is dead and gone...gone with the wind...oh, oh, oh!" The Duchess stiffened, turned white and pointed at the box that contained Sweetums.

"My goodness," the Queen said, "Ruthie, are you all right? You look as if you've seen a ghost."

The Duchess stabbed an index finger at the embroidery box. "It is moving! Sweetums is alive!"

As if tugged by a ghost, the embroidery box was moving inexplicably, drifting toward the edge of the table.

"Well, I never!" the Queen jumped up and snatched the box, "You get out of here! You scat!" She yelled at the monkey, and, terrified, it fled out the open door. It had somehow sneaked into the Duchess's room and tried to make off with the embroidery box containing the dead parrot.

The Duchess shrieked, "He killed Sweetums, and now he is back to kill me!"

"Oh, that animal!" said the Queen. "He is absolutely shameless." Her Majesty closed the door.

"Whew," Beth said. She was sitting on her heels. "That was close. You think she saw us?"

Beth, Bridget, and Babette had been hiding outside the Duchess's room eavesdropping.

"I don't think so," Bridget said. "But that monkey just about jumped on me!"

The monkey had run out of the Duchess's room at high speed and bounded off down the corridor. It was nowhere in sight.

Babette sighed, "Poor Madame Ruthie. You don't think the Guard really trained his monkey to attack her parrot, do you?"

"Of course not," Bridget said. "What sort of crazy nut would do something like that?"

"I don't know," the French girl adjusted her sunglasses. "Men are capable of strange things, especially when they are in love."

"In love?" Bridget looked at Babette. Could the French girl possibly be right? The Guard in love with the Duchess? But if he was, why didn't he propose? Why leave the poor woman hanging?

"Well, I've had it with this mystery," Beth stood to her feet. "Come on, you guys."

The tall girl strode off down the hallway. She walked so rapidly that her thick braid bounced up and down between her shoulder blades.

Babette and Bridget had to run to catch up.

Bridget yelled, "Where are we going, Beth? Are we trailing the monkey?"

"If there is one thing that makes me mad," Beth said, "it is men who break the hearts of poor defenseless women like Ruthie. We are going to the Guard's quarters. We are going to confront him face to face and find out if he loves Ruthie or not!"

As they walked along, Bridget wiggled her fingers—a sure sign that she was thinking. As they rounded a corner, she said, "I saw this movie once, or maybe it was a soap opera. There was this guy who got hit on the head and developed amnesia. Just like the Guard."

"Must have been a soap," Beth said. "In soaps, amnesia is practically an epidemic."

"What happened was, the guy got banged on the head a second time and got his memory back."

Babette smiled, "Really, Bridget, you do not plan to hit the poor man over the head, I hope."

"Well, maybe," Bridget said, "if all else fails!"

The girls arrived at a locked door.

Beth paused in front of it. "You guys ready for another spelling test? This door's got a computer lock; the Guard programmed it. We can't enter this wing of the Palace until we pass the test." She pushed a green button. "It's voice activated; this computer can talk."

"Who is it?" the computer asked. It had a rather snotty voice, sort of like the Guard's voice but speeded up.

"You know who it is," Beth said. "Give us the test."

"Three people, three words," the computer said. "Easy, difficult, or fiendishly difficult?"

"Fiendishly difficult!" Bridget shouted.

The other two gave her a dirty look.

"Hey, don't you guys like a challenge?" Bridget looked a little guilty.

Babette had wanted to ask for easy words. Even Beth, who was a good speller, had planned to ask for difficult. She hoped they would not be stuck here all day trying to get past the computer lock.

"Fiendishly difficult word number one," the computer said. It made a little sniff.

"Who wants to be first?" Beth asked.

"Lay it on me!" Bridget said confidently.

The computer made a whirring noise. "Word number one is PAMPHLET."

Bridget had to think about the word; she knew darn well there was something tricky about it. It sounded as if it were spelled PAMFLET. She visualized that spelling in her mind, but it didn't look right. Suddenly, she remembered that the word PAMPHLET has a silent H. "Here goes," she pulled down hard on her baseball cap and spelled, "P–A–M–P–H," she said the H especially loudly, "L–E–T!"

"Correct!" said the computer.

Bridget grinned. She got a big kick out of spelling hard words correctly, and fiendishly difficult words were *especially* fun to spell.

"Fiendishly difficult word number two," the computer said.

"If you do not mind, Beth," Babette murmured, "I will go next."

"Word number two is—PERSISTENT."

"Oh, dear," the French girl whispered. This wasn't going to be easy. She wondered if the first syllable might be spelled PURR, as in a cat's purr. No, she decided. Very likely it was a PER word—like *PERSON* or *PERCENTAGE*. What a horribly difficult language English is! Babette spelled, "P–E–R–S–I–S." She got that far and stopped. Could it end with TANT?

Bridget knew very well how to spell the word PERSISTENT; she wanted in the worst way to help her friend. Maybe if she made a sort of TENT with her hands? But no, it would be cheating. She closed her eyes and sent some good vibrations in her friend's direction.

"T–E–N–T," Babette said. "*Oui*, that is right, I hope. P–E–R–S–I–S–T–E–N–T!"

The computer beeped twice, then said, "Correct!"

Bridget whooped happily and waved her fist in the air to encourage Babette. "You go, girl!"

"Fiendishly difficult word number three," the computer said.

"Take your best shot," Beth said. The tall girl had a determined look on her face.

The computer whirred for a moment as if it were looking through all of its programs for an especially difficult word. "Word number three is—PERSONNEL."

Bridget popped a piece of bubble gum in her mouth and chewed it as hard as she could. She hoped Beth knew how to spell the word. It was very easy to get it confused with the word PERSONAL. The word PERSONNEL has the emphasis on the last syllable (nel), while PERSONAL has the emphasis on the first syllable (per).

Beth took a deep breath and rapidly spelled the word. She got every single letter right! "P–E–R–S–O–N–N–E–L."

The computer beeped six times in a row and said, "Correct!" The locked door made a loud grinding nose and sprang open.

"Let's go," Beth told the other two. "The Guard's room is right down this hall and around that corner."

The girls ran around the corner and practically fell over Barnaby and Biff. The boys were standing directly in front of the Guard's room. It, too, had one of those computer locks. Barnaby and Biff looked sort of angry and frustrated.

"The King's in there with Sir Pete," Biff whispered. "Where've you guys been?"

"Never you mind," Beth told her brother. "Why don't you go in?"

"All we know is that the King is angry."

"But Pop never gets angry," Beth said.

"He's so angry that steam is shooting out of his ears."

"Well, open the door," Bridget said. "We have to find out what's happening!"

Biff looked at Barnaby. "We're sort of stuck, actually."

Barnaby nodded. "We can't get in—we can't spell all the words." He pointed at the computer lock on the door to the Guard's room.

"What words?" Bridget demanded.

"The computer said we had to spell four fiendishly difficult words."

"We spelled three of them—no problem!" Biff said.

Barnaby said the words they had spelled correctly, "RECEIVE, REPETITION, and STATIONARY."

"Wow, those are pretty tough ones," Beth agreed.

Biff nodded. "No kidding. But we missed the last one."

"I can't figure it out," Barnaby said. "I was sure we got it right."

"What was the last word?" Bridget demanded.

"MARRIAGE," Biff said.

Beth looked at Bridget. Bridget stared right back at her.

"I can't believe I screwed up," Barnaby said.

Beth asked, "So, how'd you spell it?"

Barnaby leaned over so that his mouth was close to the computer lock and spelled, "M–A–R–R–I–A–G–E."

The computer beeped, then said, "Incorrect! No admittance!"

"I am absolutely sure that is how you spell it," Barnaby said. "I just can't figure this out—it's like the computer lock is broken or something."

Bridget looked at the other girls, "Are you guys thinking what I'm thinking?"

Beth nodded. Babette grinned.

"Remember what we heard the Duchess tell the Queen?" Babette said. She smiled at Bridget and Beth, "There is only one word the Guard misspells."

"Yeah," Bridget said, "he spells every word in the universe right, except one: MARRIAGE. The Duchess figures it's a sign." She winked at Beth and pointed at the computer lock. "You want to do the honors?"

Beth leaned over to the computer and misspelled MARRIAGE the way the Guard always misspelled it. She left out the i and said, "M–A–R–R–A–G–E!"

The computer whirred, beeped twice, and said, "Correct!" Even computers can be wrong sometimes.

The kids cheered. The Guard had made a mistake with his own spellchecker!

"I guess everybody really does misspell a few words," Biff said.

The door to the Guard's room whirred loudly and sprang open.

The kids were about to enter, but before they got a foot inside the doorway, they were almost knocked over.

The King was angry all right. That nice man who seemed never to stop smiling, who was just about as kind and friendly as Santa Claus, had hold of the Guard of Spelling's ear and was dragging the poor man out of his room!

"Pete, you're coming with me! We're going to straighten this out once and for all!" the King yelled. "I order you to tell Ruthie the entire story!"

Aa Bb Cc Dd Ee Ff Gg Hh Ii Jj

Exercises for Chapter 14

More Fiendishly Difficult Words from Sir Pete's Word Hoard

MARRIAGE—the one word that Sir Pete can't spell! It has two Rs; and don't forget the I. Don't misspell it like the computer did: MARRAGE.

NUCLEAR—this is one of the very tricky words. It may help to remember that NUCLEAR ends with the word CLEAR. Don't misspell it NUCULAR.

PAMPHLET—as Bridget knew, this word is tricky because it contains a silent H. Remember that PH makes an F sound. Don't misspell it PAMFLET.

PERSISTENT—this is the one that gave Babette a little trouble. PER–SIS–TENT. It may help to think of your sister (SIS) in a TENT. Don't misspell it PURSISTANT.

PERSONNEL/PERSONAL—these two words are easy to mix up. PERSONNEL means *the persons employed by an organization or company*. It also refers to the part of an organization that is concerned with all the employees. "We have a lot of personnel problems in our school. Jack thinks that personnel need to hire some more teachers." PERSONAL means *of a particular person* or *private*. "Don't mention her bad breath—it's too personal!" Both words start with PERSON, but the endings are different. PERSONNEL has an extra N and ends with EL. PERSONAL has only one N and ends with AL.

RECEIVE—remember the Duchess's rule, I Before E Except After C? This is a good example of this rule. Don't misspell it RECIEVE.

REPETITION—it may help to remember that this word contains the word PET in the middle. To teach my PET a trick, I have to use a lot of REPETITION.

SIMILAR—the ending is the tricky part. AR, not ER. Don't misspell it SIMALER.

SKILLFUL—the root word is SKILL. Don't forget the second L. The last syllable FUL has only one L. Don't misspell it SKILFULL.

STATIONARY/STATIONERY—the root word is STATION. The TION (pronounced SHUN) can be tricky. Also watch out for the ending: The word that ends in ARY means *standing still in one place*; the word that ends in ERY means *writing paper*. Here's a hint: ENVELOPE begins with an E, you put STATION*E*RY in an *ENVE-LOPE*.

WEATHER/WHETHER—these words are easy to confuse. When we talk about things like snow and rain, we are talking about WEATHER. Don't forget the A. WHETHER means *if it* or *whatever is the case.* "Do you know whether the library is open?" "Whether by luck or skill, all I know is he won the race." Remember that WHETHER has two Hs.

Find and correct the errors in the following sentences. The number of mistakes is in parentheses at the end of the sentences.

1. My grandparents have the world's most perfect marrage. (1)

2. Pepe and Selina were standing on the corner passing out pamflets against nucular war. (2)

3. Dad always says if you are pursistant, you will eventually recieve your reward. (2)

4. Don't take it to personnel, but you need to wipe your nose. (2)

5. If you want to be skilfull, it takes endless repitition. (2)

6. This statshunary is very simaler to that stationery. (3)

7. Weather or not we go to the beach depends on the whether. (2)

8. My mom runs the Personal Department and she just recieved a big raise. (2)

9. If that nucular bomb blows up, we're all dead! (1)

10. She has a personel problem; her marrage is going badly. (2)

11. The wether man said the cold front will be stationery for the next twelve hours. (2)

12. Alicia persistantly recieves the highest grades in our class. (2)

13. Where'd I put that pamplet about camping in the Ozarks? (1)

14. Wether we win or not depends on how skilfull we are. (2)

15. Their marrages are sort of simalur— fantastic! (2)

see page 254 for answers

Chapter 15:
The Funeral of Sweetums

Say these rules over and over out loud: "No English words end with *V*! After *Q* comes *U*! *I* Before *E* Except After *C.*"

On top of the wall that ran around the Palace garden, Beauregard had just declared his love for Cleopatra. The white cat turned her back on Beauregard and looked back at him over her shoulder and slowly waved her tail, which meant in cat language that she found him kind of cute. In the midst of his happiness, Beauregard noticed something a little strange—a monkey perched in an apple tree. It was the very same monkey that had ripped the tail feathers out of the parrot. Beauregard wondered momentarily what sort of mischief the animal might be up to now, but Cleopatra half-closed her eyes and stretched out her front paws in a way that was so darn beautiful that he forgot all about the monkey and concentrated on the pretty cat.

The apple tree had a large branch that jutted out at a right angle, and that was where the monkey was sitting. He seemed to be examining the fur on his shoulder (possibly for fleas), but in fact his attention was carefully fixed on two women who had just finished digging a hole in the garden.

The Duchess and the Queen were nearly ready to bury Sweetums. The unfortunate parrot was in Lady Ruthie's embroidery box, which had been transformed into an elegant coffin. Tied up in a black ribbon, the hand-painted box was on the grass not far from the hole the two women had just dug.

Her Majesty laid down her garden spade, then put her hands on her hips and looked at the Duchess. The Lady Ruthie looked at the embroidery box and sighed heavily.

"Ruthie," her Majesty said kindly, "would you like to say a few words?"

The Duchess seemed ready to make a speech about her parrot when she heard a noise. She stopped before she even got out a single word and looked back toward the Palace. The noise coming from just inside the Palace was so loud that Beauregard and Cleopatra looked up, too. Even the monkey looked up from his perch in the apple tree.

The door that led from the Palace into the garden flew open.

"Well, I never...," said the Queen.

"Can that be the King?" the Duchess said in amazement.

Normally, his Majesty was a very even-tempered man. On most occasions, he was likely to be smiling. The King had twinkly eyes and a wonderful disposition. He was plump and jolly, the sort of man who seems to be just what you would want if you could order up a nice old grandfather. But on this occasion, the King did not look happy. He frowned ferociously, his jaw stuck out, and his eyes blazed.

"He's got hold of the Guard!" the Duchess said.

"By the ear!" her Majesty said.

It seemed perfectly astounding. The King had hold of Sir Pete by the ear and was hauling him into the garden. They were not alone, either. Behind them was a trail of kids and the giant dog Woof. Woof was high stepping; his tail was whipping from side to side, and he was barking loudly and frequently.

"Ah, there they are!" the King said. He let go of Sir Pete's ear. "You see them over there, Pete?"

Sir Pete rubbed his ear. The upper half of it had turned bright red. He did not look at all happy. But he did not look mad either. He looked scared and ashamed.

"Woof, hush up," the King said. The huge dog sat down on the grass. "Pete, I mean it," his Majesty folded his arms and gave the Guard a hard look, "do your duty."

Sir Pete hung his head. He seemed deeply ashamed of himself.

The monkey crept higher up the tree branch. He seemed a little afraid of Woof. Then he looked thoughtfully at the embroidery box.

"Go to her, Pete," the King demanded. "Tell her the truth, the whole truth!"

Beth, Babette, and Bridget watched all this carefully. Beth and Babette were excited to see the conclusion of the mystery. They were certain that they were going to find out what had really happened the day the Guard of Spelling had gotten hit on the head by Ruthie's dictionary. From their perch on top of the wall, Beauregard and Cleopatra watched. Woof watched. Barnaby and Biff watched.

Since nobody was paying him the slightest attention, the monkey started to climb down from the tree. He descended very slowly so that no one would notice him.

When the Duchess saw the Guard, she became so flustered that she turned red. Her Majesty drew back a few steps so that Sir Pete and the Duchess could have a little privacy.

Sir Pete walked right up to Ruthie, took off his helmet, and bowed. He did not seem to want to look the Duchess in the eye. His hand darted into his breastplate and pulled something out, something that looked like a dead cat.

"Oh, no," Beth groaned, "it's Ruthie's wig. He's saved it."

The Guard bowed to the Duchess, then handed her the wig. It was in pretty awful shape and looked as if someone had used it to mop a floor.

The Duchess snatched her wig from his hand. While the Guard looked delicately in another direction, she put the wig back on top of her head so that it resembled a Russian fur cap.

After using both hands to adjust her wig, Ruthie turned pale but drew herself to her full height. "Sir, have you come to torment me? Have you not hurt me often enough?"

Sir Pete fell to his knees. "I beg your pardon, Ruthie. I'd like to strangle the darn monkey if only I could get my hands on him."

In the apple tree, the monkey had arrived at the very lowest branch. When he realized that everyone was looking at him, the monkey made an outrageous noise, then fell to the ground and picked himself up, all the while trying to appear completely innocent.

Everyone else turned his or her attention back to the Guard and the Duchess.

The Guard twisted his pie-plate helmet around and around in his hands as if he would like to throw it somewhere. "Ruthie, I'm here to apologize for the death of Sweetums. I know how much you cared for that bird. He was a fine parrot."

Ruthie dabbed her eyes. She looked sadly at the embroidery box.

"I know there's nothing I can say to make you feel any better."

The Duchess took a deep breath. She looked directly at Sir Pete and said, "Sir, I want you to know I am leaving the Palace forever."

Sir Pete looked plainly surprised.

"You will not have me to kick around, not any more, Sir. My heart is broken."

The Guard turned bright red. He took a deep breath. "Ruthie, you have to let me say this. I don't blame you for wanting to leave. I've been a coward—that is the right word. A coward all right. Worse than that. I've been a dirty dog, lowdown as a snake. Compared to me, a snake is an upstanding citizen. I've been lying to you." His lower lip quivered. "There's no way you can ever forgive me. I am the one who should clear out of here."

The Duchess seemed touched by this speech. She raised her hand to stop him from saying any more. "Sir, you may have your failings; you certainly do, but they are mostly due to the accident to your poor brain, which in a way is all my fault. Don't think I have forgotten that fact. But I know you to be a gentleman, and never a liar. Why, Sir Pete, you are honest as..." The Duchess waved her hand in the air and seemed unable to think of anything quite as honest as Sir Pete.

He hung his head and twisted the helmet. "I'm the worst sort of cowardly liar there is."

The Duchess seemed confused. "How so?"

Everyone leaned forward to hear the Guard's answer.

"After your book, your dictionary, hit me on the head, I only pretended to have amnesia."

The Duchess jumped as if she had been shocked. "Pretended?!"

"The truth is, I only lost my nerve. I've been a bachelor for a long time, all of my life. A woman as grand as you, a rare beauty like you, raised by the finest people, the sister of a King, you're about ten times too fine for the likes of me, Ruthie. Until my sister got me this job here at the Palace, I was nothing but a nobody from nowhere, no good to anyone, an embarrassment to my family."

The Duchess moved much closer to Sir Pete. "Don't say such things! You are a valuable person. Why without you, English spelling would just fly all to pieces!"

The Guard hung his head. "Ruthie, I have to tell you what happened that day. After I proposed and you accepted, I jumped up. My head hit the shelf and that dictionary hit me square on the head. I lay there on the floor after the book hit me and I thought of marriage, happiness, respectability, and I completely lost my nerve. I mean, who was I kidding? To dream of marrying someone as fine and decent as you? Ruthie, I pretended to have amnesia." He looked up at her woefully. "It was just a lie. I am just about as fake as a three-dollar bill. I pretended that I forgot I had proposed, forgot how I loved you."

"Pretended? You just pretended? You never had amnesia? Never, Sir Pete?"

"Everyone seemed willing to go along with it—but afterward, I am telling you, Ruthie, I felt the worst sort of guilt you can imagine. I've suffered every day of it, living a lie is the worst life there is. And that's the sorry truth." He took a deep breath. "So if anybody's leaving the Palace in disgrace and never coming back, it's me. Not you."

All the time Sir Pete was making this speech, the monkey was creeping toward the open grave. He often stopped to sniff blades of grass and flowers, and was not noticed by anyone—except perhaps by Woof. The big dog had laid his enormous head on his paws. His eyes were half-closed and he seemed almost asleep, but in fact, Woof was keeping an eye on the monkey.

The Duchess Ruthie held her hand to her mouth. She seemed amazed, almost speechless. "Sir Pete, it was all an act? You never had amnesia, not at any time?"

"Not even for one second." Sir Pete got to his feet. "Ruthie, if you would like to give me a good kick, go ahead. I deserve it. Or if it would relieve your feelings at all to hit me hard on the noggin with a lead pipe, or strike me several times with a baseball bat—anything of that sort is only what I deserve." He closed his mouth and hung his head; his big hands twisted the helmet around and around.

There was a long pause. The Duchess seemed lost in thought.

While everyone waited for the Duchess to say something in response to Sir Pete's surprising confession, behind the Queen, behind Sir Pete and the Lady Ruthie, the monkey sneaked up to the mouth of the open grave and dove in. No one noticed him except Woof. The dog lifted up his head, sniffed, then stood up and took a couple steps forward.

"Don't you bother them, Woofie," the King whispered. "Let them get it all settled."

Woof looked back at the King, wrinkled the skin along his nose in dissatisfaction, then obediently sat down in the grass.

"I mean it, Ruthie," the Guard looked up at the Duchess, "before I go, if you want to bang me hard over the head with a tree branch, it's only fair." He hung his head again. "I know you won't ever want to see me again or even hear mention of my name. But, just remember that I have always and will always love you."

The Duchess turned her face away from him.

Behind the Queen, the monkey peeked up out of the grave. His black, bright eyes gleamed with mischief. He ducked back into the grave, disappearing from view entirely. Then from the grave, a long black arm emerged and groped the grass beside the grave until it touched the embroidery box.

Woof stood to his feet and looked back at the King, who had all his attention fixed on the Duchess and the Guard.

"I won't deny that I am angry," the Duchess said. She did not turn to look at Sir Pete. "And hurt. But that is too much. I would never hurt you. And I don't want you to leave. Leave his Majesty—and your sister? It wouldn't be right. I'm the one to go."

"Ruthie," the Guard whispered, "I can't let you be the one to leave. I'm the one who did wrong, not you." The Guard put his helmet back on his head. He turned to the Queen. "Sis, I'm going. I'm heading for distant parts. I don't know where. But when I get there, I'll send you a postcard. I want to thank you for everything. You have been a wonderful sister in every way."

The Queen took a step toward him and looked at the Duchess. "Oh, Pete," she said softly.

Babette took off her sunglasses and wiped away a tear. This was the saddest thing she'd ever seen.

The Guard and the Duchess turned their backs to one another. They seemed ready to part forever. The Queen looked helplessly at the King. Beth looked at Babette. Barnaby looked at Biff. Cleopatra looked at Beauregard. Somebody had to do something!

"Pete!" the Duchess cried. "You can't go!"

The Guard spun around and looked hard at the Duchess. She looked hard at him. Then they both ran to one another and embraced!

We probably do not need to describe everything else that happened. The Guard proposed again, and Ruthie accepted again. And this time when they kissed, no Dictionary of Rationalized Spelling fell from the skies to hit anyone in the head. The kids and the King and Queen crowded around Pete and Ruthie to congratulate them. Everyone hugged and kissed and wept and laughed.

Inside the grave, the monkey crouched down and eagerly untied the black ribbon around the embroidery box. He pulled off the lid of the box and started to unwrap the black silk that was wound around the body of the parrot. The monkey's eyes gleamed with excitement. Then something seized the monkey by his long tail and yanked him right up out of the grave!

Woof had entertained dark suspicions about the monkey from the first time he had seen the animal sneaking across the lawn. While everyone else had been jumping up and down with excitement and congratulating Lady Ruthie and Sir Pete, the giant dog trotted over to the open grave and discovered the monkey. With his teeth, Woof grabbed the animal by the tail, yanked him from the grave, and began to trot around the garden, hoping one of the humans might notice that a monkey was dangling like a toy from his jaws. Woof rapidly circled the crowd of people clustered around Ruthie and the Guard of Spelling. He made several loud yips but held tightly onto the monkey's tail.

The monkey shrieked and held tightly to the box.

The parrot began to bounce up and down in its wooden box.

It is time to reveal a secret. After the monkey had torn out its last two tail feathers and Sweetums had flown over the auditorium into a restroom and collided with a mirror, it had fallen legs up into a sink. At that moment, Sweetums had certainly looked dead. When the Lady Ruthie had discovered her bird in that position, not moving, not even breathing, she had supposed that it *was* dead. She'd clutched Sweetums to her breast and run weeping to her room. But the parrot was not dead. He was only stunned.

The parrot awakened lying on its back in a wooden box. Right above its head were the bright eyes and grimacing mouth of that monkey! And just above the monkey was the huge head and long teeth of that giant dog!

The parrot screamed and leapt out of the embroidery box. At least he *tried* to leap out, but the box was so small that the bird's wings got stuck. Sweetums fell from the box and screamed like a siren. Woof was so startled to hear the noise that he came to an abrupt halt. The parrot's cries so startled the monkey that it, too, screamed. Everyone stopped congratulating Sir Pete and Lady Ruthie and turned around to see what was going on. They saw a most amazing sight.

The parrot tried to fly. It spread its wings and threw itself into the air. The monkey grabbed one of its legs. Woof held tightly to the monkey's tail. Flapping wildly, the parrot rose three feet into the air. The monkey was stretched between the parrot and Woof. The huge dog had the monkey's tail in his mouth, and the monkey had his hand clenched around the parrot's leg. The bird flapped his wings as violently as he had ever flapped in his life. The monkey would not let go. Woof would not let go.

"For heaven's sake!" the Queen cried.

"Woof!" yelled the King. "You let go this minute!"

Woof let go. The monkey fell to the ground; he would not let go of Sweetums. Flapping wildly and shrieking loudly, the parrot dragged the monkey along the ground over flowers and plants until they both crashed into a bush. Then Sweetums turned his head and, with his long beak, bit the monkey on the finger. He bit him hard!

The monkey screamed and popped his wounded finger in his mouth, and then jumped into the bush hoping that no one would catch and punish him.

"Sweetums!" cried the Duchess. She ran to save her bird, who was now striding triumphantly up and down on the lawn in front of the bush where the monkey was hiding. "You're not dead!" The Duchess gathered up the parrot and held him cradled in her arm like a baby. "Sweetums, you're alive!"

"*I Before E,*" the parrot said thoughtfully.

"How do you like that?" Beth said to Babette. "The bird's alive, the monkey got his punishment, and Ruthie and Pete are going to get married. Now, that's what I call a happy ending!"

"No English words end with *V*," Sweetums said. "After *Q* comes *U*! *I Before E, I Before E Except After C.*"

Exercises for Chapter 15

While the monkey's finger heals up, the parrot grows some new tail feathers, and the Duchess of Rules and the Guard of Spelling plan their wedding, let's see if we can learn some more of the difficult words in Sir Pete's Word Hoard.

ANALYSIS—it helps to pronounce this one slowly: AN–AL–Y–SIS. That Y is tricky!

APPARENT—contains the word PARENT and has two *P*s. Don't misspell it APARUNT.

APPEARANCE—has two *P*s. Contains the word PEAR. It is an ANCE word, not an ENCE word. Don't misspell it APPEERENCE.

ARRANGEMENT—has two *R*s, contains the word RANGE. AR–RANGE–MENT.

BENEFIT/BENEFITTED—notice that the UH sound in the middle is an *E*, not an *A*. BEN–E–FIT. Don't misspell it BENAFIT. The past tense has two *T*s.

CANCEL—don't misspell it CANCUL.

CONFIDENT—contains the word DENT; don't misspell it CONFIDUNT.

CONTROVERSY—say it slowly: CON–TRO–VERS–Y. Don't put a U in it. The last part is tricky. Don't misspell the word CONTROVURSY.

CRITICISM—starts with the word CRITIC, and remember that it is an ISM word. Don't put a K in it.

DESPERATE—the last two syllables are tricky. The *purr* sound is spelled PER; the ending is ATE, not IT. Don't misspell it DESPURIT.

DISAPPOINT—has only one S, and don't forget that second P. Contains the word POINT. The *uh* sound is spelled with an A this time. DIS–AP–POINT.

ELIGIBLE—it is very easy to leave out that first I. Don't misspell it ELGIBLE. Notice that there are no As in this word. EL–I–GI–BLE.

Find and correct the mistakes in the following sentences. The number of mistakes is in parentheses at the end of the sentences.

1. According to Maria's analisis, this arangement benefitted no one. (3)

2. How can I put this gently? Your apearence was a little disapointing. (2)

3. Can you take a little critacism? (1)

4. They cancelled the swim meet. Roseann was really disapointed. (1)

5. There's a big controvursy over who is elgible to win the contest. (2)

6. Joanna is really confidunt that her arangment is the best. (2)

7. It was aparent early that Ling was despurat. (2)

8. She gets depressed if she gets even the slightest critacizm. (1)

9. My dad was really disapointted when we lost the big game. (1)

Aa Bb Cc Dd Ee Ff Gg Hh Ii

10. Who says boys aren't elgible? Anyone can try out for the eighth grade play! (1)

11. We're supposed to write about some big social controvursey like abortion or euthanasia. (1)

12. After a lot of scientific anallysis, they found out the river was dangerously polluted. (1)

13. Aparently, her apeerence at the circus caused a sensation. (2)

14. She's going out with Zack? She must be totally desperit! (1)

see page 255 for answers

Chapter 16:
The Wedding

Testing yourself
is a great
way to learn
how to spell!

Barnaby cleared his throat, then poked Bridget in the ribs. "You have to admit Chick the Chicken King sure knows how to throw a wedding!"

The reason that Barnaby had to poke Bridget in the ribs with his finger was that she was not paying him much attention. She was gazing with fascination at the giant hot air balloon that was tethered on one side of the Palace rose garden.

It was the Chicken King's trademark balloon, the one the fabulously successful businessman used when he participated in hot air balloon races. The Chicken King was very fond of hot air balloon races and had even won a couple of them. His balloon was shaped like an enormous bucket of fried chicken. On its sides were the Chicken King trademark, a huge picture of the Chicken King in his chicken costume. But today, the balloon looked a little different. The Chicken King had ordered some modifications. New pieces of special cloth were stretched like banners over the Chicken King trademark. On one side of the balloon, JUST MARRIED! was written in huge letters. On the other side was written PETE + RUTHIE = LOVE.

When the Chicken King had heard that Sir Pete and the Lady Ruthie were getting married, he happily picked up all the expenses. When he was a boy, the King and Queen had been his favorite teachers, and he never tired of giving them, or anyone related to them, nice things.

The rose garden was full of hundreds of bouquets of flowers.

"It looks like he bought out an entire flower store," Bridget said. "Maybe two of them!"

"You could not have a better day for a wedding," Babette told Beauregard.

It was an absolutely perfect day, mild and sunny. A breeze was blowing just hard enough to keep the big balloon bobbing slightly on its ropes. An entire orchestra was crowded into one corner of the garden and played one love song after another. At least two hundred folding chairs had been set up in rows that were separated by an aisle. A line of tables was arranged in the shade near the Palace wall. Each table was full of food. Behind each table was a chef. All of this was provided by the generous Chicken King.

"Pretty good crowd," Beauregard said. In fact, every chair was filled. All the friends of Pete and Ruthie were there. Lots of kids who loved to come to the Palace to read and write were sitting on both sides of the aisle. All of them were excited to see the wedding. The fact that they were all going to get to take a ride in the Chicken King's hot air balloon after the ceremony was pretty exciting, too!

Bridget's parents were sitting just to the left of Bridget, Babette, Barnaby, and Beauregard. Cleopatra was there, as well as another dozen cats. Woof was lying on the grass not too far from the tables of food. Beside the giant dog, a half dozen German shepherds and three Labradors lounged on the grass.

Everyone was on his or her best behavior. The older people, the kids, the dogs and cats—every single person in attendance— was wearing one of the Chicken King's trademark bright red caps.

The Chicken King was striding back and forth in front of all the chairs. He was eager to get going. Chick was the sort of person who is always eager to get going. It was not hard to pick him out of the crowd because he was wearing his rooster suit. Chick loved that suit and wore it on all formal occasions.

"Look at him," Barnaby said, "sometimes I think that guy is turning into a chicken!"

The Chicken King clucked; he scratched the ground with his big yellow chicken feet; he flapped his wings and emitted a loud cockadoodledoo!

Bridget said, "He's going to perform the ceremony, can you believe it? Imagine getting married by a guy in a rooster suit!"

"He's not just any guy in a rooster suit," Babette observed. "He's Chick the Chicken King."

"Among other things, he's a licensed minister, that's what the Queen says," Barnaby explained. "That's why he can marry them."

Bridget pointed. "Hey, look at Sir Pete. The poor guy looks scared to death."

The Guard of Spelling was wearing brand new armor. It was polished until it shined like silvery chrome. When the sun caught Sir Pete just right, you had to squint or else get blinded.

"You don't think Sir Pete's going to faint or something, do you?" Bridget asked.

Although the Guard sometimes seemed a little ferocious, in fact he was a rather shy individual. His jaw was clenched. He paced back and forth in a circle right in front of everyone. His forehead was covered with beads of sweat. His cheeks were flushed.

"I think it's just nerves," Barnaby rubbed his bushy hair with one hand. "Every guy who's about to get married looks just like that—scared to death!" Barnaby was just about to tell the others about one of his uncles who had gotten so nervous at his wedding that he had broken out in hives, but the others shushed him.

"Shh!" Bridget waved her hand at Barnaby to shut up. "It's starting!"

The orchestra started playing another love song.

Wearing a white tuxedo, Biff came out from behind a large rose bush and took up his position beside the Guard.

"Wow, look at that," Bridget said. "Biff's the best man." She thought he looked absolutely fabulous in his cool tux.

Babette leaned over to her and whispered, "Beth's the maid of honor."

"I wonder who the flower girl is," Bridget whispered. She turned in her seat and craned her neck to see who was coming out of the back door of the Palace. "Flower girls are always so little and cute that I just love them!"

When the flower girl emerged from the door, everyone in the rose garden made a little gasp. People popped their hands over their mouths to keep them from laughing out loud.

The flower girl was carrying a bouquet of roses and carnations so large that she nearly disappeared behind it. She was wearing a lovely pale green dress that was very short and frilly. On her head sat a huge, shiny bow.

Barnaby had to pinch the bridge of his nose to keep from laughing. Even Babette could not repress a smile. Bridget had to slap both her hands over her mouth or she would have roared.

The flowergirl's black hairy arms and legs stuck out of the perfectly beautiful frock. It was the monkey!

Its tail displayed a large white bandage. Apparently the parrot had gotten a little more revenge for the loss of his tail feathers.

The door opened again and the ring bearer emerged. It was the parrot, of course. Sweetums walked slowly, more or less in time with the music. The brilliant green parrot wore a tam on its head, and in the middle of the tam, a piece of golden thread held a golden wedding ring.

The hairy "flower girl" took up his position beside the Guard of Spelling and Biff. The parrot wobbled up the aisle and came to a stop not far behind the monkey.

The door opened again, and Beth emerged. She was wearing an absolutely gorgeous gown the same color as the dress worn by the monkey.

As soon as Beth arrived at the front with the others, the music stopped and then started up again. The orchestra played "Here Comes the Bride." The back door of the Palace swung open and out came Ruthie, the Duchess of Rules, dressed in a long, elaborate wedding gown with a big veil.

"Hey, that gown is really fabulous," Bridget said, "but isn't it sort of dirty or something?"

The gown appeared to be spotted and streaked. Everyone strained to see what it was.

"Words!" Babette lifted her sunglasses so she could see better. "Mademoiselle Ruthie's gown is covered with spelling words."

"Hard ones!" Barnaby said.

As the Duchess came down the center aisle, Barnaby was able to read some of the spelling words written on her gown. "BARBECUE. Now that is a tough one. I always think there is a Q in it."

"ARCTIC," Babette read. The word was written across the Duchess's shoulder. "It's really easy to leave out that middle C."

As the Duchess passed them, Bridget read the words DEFI-NITELY and FULFILL written on the right side of the gown. The word OCCASION ran across the Duchess's shoulders.

At the left side of the Duchess, holding her arm, was the King. At her other side was the Queen. Since her parents were deceased, the Duchess was being given away by her brother, his Majesty, and by her best friend, her Majesty. All of them were smiling ear to ear, beaming in the bright sunlight.

"Who gives away this woman?" Chick the Chicken King demanded in his most serious voice.

"We do!" answered the King and the Queen. They took their seats in the first row of folding chairs. Her Majesty wiped away a tear, and his Majesty patted her hand.

The Chicken King was about to begin by making a little speech, but the Guard of Spelling stopped him. "Ruthie," he said, "I've got something to say to you." He lifted back the Lady Ruthie's veil, revealing her beaming face.

"Uh-oh," Bridget whispered. Was it possible? Was the Guard going to back out at the last minute?

"In my whole career as the Guard of Spelling, I've only messed up one spelling word."

"MARRIAGE," whispered Barnaby.

"I guess everyone here knows which one. Well, I want you and all these people to know that I now know how to spell MARRIAGE. You've got to remember to put the I in it!" He patted himself on the breastplate. "M–A–R–R–I–A–G–E!"

"Cockadoodledoo!" crowed the Chicken King.

After that, the ceremony went off without a hitch.

"Do you take this man to be your wedded husband?" the Chicken King asked.

The parrot spelled out the word, "HUSBAND, H–U–S–B–A–N–D."

"I do!" the Duchess said in a loud voice.

The Chicken King turned to the Guard of Spelling. He gave his bright red comb a shake. "Pete, do you take this woman to be your wife?"

"WIFE, W–I–F–E," spelled the parrot.

Pete stood up very straight. He looked scared. He turned pale as a ghost. Was he going to faint?

Then he suddenly whooped and in a very loud voice yelled, "I certainly do—now and forever! For better or worse, I take you, Ruthie, to be my wedded wife. You bet I do!"

"Was that a yes?" the Chicken King asked, grinning a little.

"Yes!" yelled the Guard. "Yes, I do take her! A million times, yes!"

The Chicken King smiled broadly, "Then I pronounce you man and wife." He threw back his head and yelled, "Cockadoodledoo!"

Ruthie and Pete stared at each other and both of them grinned goofy grins. They didn't seem to know what to do next.

"Marriage, M–A–R–R–I–A–G–E. You've got to remember to put the I in it," said the parrot.

The Chicken King reached out with his wing and whacked Pete on his armored shoulder, "Well, Pete, what are you waiting for? You may kiss the bride!"

As Pete and Ruthie kissed, the entire audience rose to their feet and cheered. A few hundred red caps flew up into the air.

"I guess that's how you spell 'happy ending,'" murmured Babette.

Aa Bb Cc Dd Ee Ff Gg Hh Ii Jj

Exercises for Chapter 16

These are the difficult spelling words that were printed on Duchess Ruthie's wedding gown. Let's see if you can learn them all.

ARCTIC—don't forget that C in the middle; there are two Cs in this word. Don't misspell it ARTIC.

ACQUAINTANCE—the first syllable AC can be tricky to remember. Notice that it ends with ANCE. AC–QUAINT–ANCE. Don't misspell it AQUAINTENCE.

BARBECUE—spell it with a C, not a Q. Don't misspell it BARBEQUE.

BURY—from BURIAL. Don't misspell it BERRY.

DEFINITELY—don't forget the E at the end. DEFI-NITE—LY. Also, remember that the word FINITE is in the middle and that there are no As in definitely. Don't misspell it DEFINATLY.

DESCRIPTION—notice the ending. This is one of the TION words. DE–SCRIP–TION.

DISCRIMINATE—notice the first syllable is DIS, not DE.

Aa Bb Cc Dd Ee Ff Gg Hh Ii

EXCEED—notice it starts EX. Don't misspell it EKSEED.

EXTENSION—It may help to remember it contains the word TENSION. Don't misspell it EKSTENSHUN.

FULFILL—remember there are only three Ls: one L, then a pair of Ls. FUL–FILL. Don't misspell it FULLFILL or FULLFIL.

OCCASION—there are no Ks in OCCASION. Remember there is a double C, but *not* a double S. Don't misspell it OKASION.

PROCEDURE—the middle syllable is tricky. PRO–CED–URE. Don't misspell it PROSEEDURE.

Aa Bb Cc Dd Ee Ff Gg Hh Ii Jj

Find and correct all the mistakes in the following sentences. The number of mistakes is in parentheses at the end of the sentences.

1. I imagine that they do not have a lot of barbeque parties in the artic. (2)

2. She's more an akquaintence than a real frend. (2)

3. We're going too berry Grandmother in the garden. (2)

4. No one is allowed to descriminate on the basis of religion or race. (1)

5. Your speed is not to ekseed 25 mph.

6. His diskription of his neighbor was hilarious. (1)

7. I'll give you a one-week ekstenshun on this assignment, but that is it. (1)

8. If you do one more project, you'll fullfil all the requirements for this class. (1)

9. On this one okasion, we're taking the harbor freeway. (1)

10. Our proseedure when we have a fire drill is for everyone to get out of the building. (1)

11. When an artick cold mass moves down from the north, it definitly gets cold. (1)

12. At the barbeque, the hotdogs were so burnt, we had to berry them. (2)

13. That deskription defenitely does him justice. (2)

14. In that whole town, I have only one akquantence. (1)

15. If there's one thing we hate at our skool, it's deskrimination. (2)

16. Mom's on the ekstension. (1)

17. We got here in one hour; Dad deafinitely ekceded the speed limit. (2)

18. On that okkasion, I just didn't feel fullfilled. (2)

19. What's our normal proseedure when someone canculs? (2)

see page 255 for answers

Chapter 17:
Really, Really Tough Spelling Test for the Entire Book

Are you ready for a really, really tough test? First, we will list all the words we have worked on in this book. Go over the entire list a few times. Pay special attention to words you had trouble learning to spell the first time. Work on them some more. Have someone—your parents, your sister, a friend, or a talking parrot—quiz you on how to spell them. Here is the entire list.

Sir Pete's Word Hoard

accept

acquaintance

actually

again

affect

a lot

always

analysis

anything

apparent

appearance

arctic

around

arrangement

assistant

athlete

attempt

barbecue

because

believe

benefit

benefited

bury

busy

buy

by

calendar

cancel

cemetery

choir

Christmas

confident

controversy

convenient

criticism

cupboard

definitely

description

desperate

diamond

didn't

difference

different

disappoint

discriminate

doesn't

don't

Easter

effect

eligible

environment

especially

everybody

everyone

everything

everywhere

exceed

except

extension

favorite

February

fiery

finally

for

foreign

forth

forty

four

fourth

friends

fulfill

gauge

government

guarantee

gypsy

Halloween

heard

height

hour

immediately

its

it's

judgment

know

laboratory

leopard

let's

license

loose

lose

loss

marriage

maybe

necessary

nickel

no

nuclear

occasion

occur

occurred

off

omit

omitted

our

paid

pamphlet

people

persistent

personal

personnel

principal

principle

probably

procedure

raspberry

really

receive

recognize

repetition

restaurant

rhythm

Saturday

sergeant

several

similar

skillful

someone

something

sometimes

sophomore

stationary

stomachache

succeed

surprise

temperature

that's

their

then

there

there's

they

they're

through

too

until

usually

vacuum

weather

went

were

we're

where

whether

which

witch

woman

women

yacht

you're

Final Exam—Exercises for All the Words in This Book

This is a truly tough final exam. It will contain all the words we have studied. It contains the 55 words that junior high students most commonly misspell, and more than 100 additional words that are frequently misspelled. Most adults misspell many of these words, so don't get upset if you miss some of them. Anyone who gets all of these right is one of the champion spellers of the universe! If you do miss some of the misspelled words or find them and fail to spell them correctly, put them on your list of words to keep studying. Use the words in sentences. Do a lot of writing, and let other people read and correct your writing. Slowly, you will get better and better. Almost no one becomes an absolutely perfect speller, but it is definitely possible to improve!

Well, here goes. Do you have a sharp pencil and an eraser? Take a deep breath and begin.

Aa Bb Cc Dd Ee Ff Gg Hh Ii Jj

THE OFFICIAL
SPELLING SMART JUNIOR
REALLY, REALLY TOUGH
SPELLING TEST

Find and correct the mistakes in the following sentences. The number of errors will be noted in parentheses at the end of the sentence. Good luck!

1. When the explosion ocurred, all the lights imediately went awf. (3)

2. He payed heavily on that okkasion. (2)

3. I wouldn't pay one nickle for enything thay sell. (3)

4. In our judgement, the director of personal here has a knack for hiring good people. (2)

5. I don't rekognize that rithum, is it Cuban? (2)

6. We won't get thru untill we make one last atempt. (3)

7. I don't care if its convenyunt or not, evry thing has to be cleared out of here! (3)

8. What diference did the lose of all his money make in his life? (2)

9. All the assembly instructions where ommitted. (2)

10. Did you receeve some thing good in the mail? (2)

11. Your right; I realy hate to loose. I take it much to personelly. (5)

12. I no ware they whent. (3)

13. She jumped from a heighth of twenty-for feet. (2)

14. That wumun has know principals at all. (3)

15. Thay think that proseedure will probly work. (3)

16. Becuz of they're apearance, they never get hired. (3)

17. We all ways fullfil the terms of the contract. (2)

18. We never exseed the speed limit akspet in an emergency. (2)

19. Witch one of those wimin was standing over thare? (3)

20. Her asistent was told to berry all the trash. (2)

21. My faverit icecream is called Razzberry Suprise. (3)

22. May be you're lepperd is unhappy, she's growling a lot. (3)

23. Lets quit using dangerous nucular power! (2)

24. To sukseed, it is neccesary to be persistant. (3)

25. Use a diferant ekstention; this one's broken. (2)

26. Does'nt frendship matter alot evrywhere? (4)

27. Weather theres enough time or not, were going to try to win this game! (3)

28. I dont beleeve we should go imediatly; lets wait untill Saterday. (6)

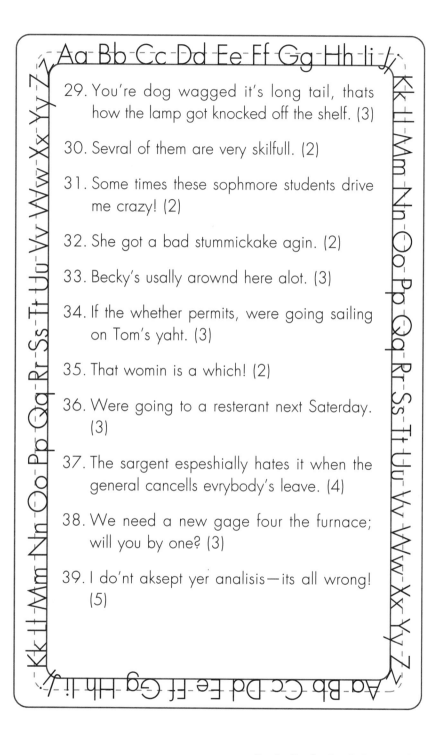

29. You're dog wagged it's long tail, thats how the lamp got knocked off the shelf. (3)

30. Sevral of them are very skilfull. (2)

31. Some times these sophmore students drive me crazy! (2)

32. She got a bad stummickake agin. (2)

33. Becky's usally arownd here alot. (3)

34. If the whether permits, were going sailing on Tom's yaht. (3)

35. That womin is a which! (2)

36. Were going to a resterant next Saterday. (3)

37. The sargent espeshially hates it when the general cancells evrybody's leave. (4)

38. We need a new gage four the furnace; will you by one? (3)

39. I do'nt aksept yer analisis—its all wrong! (5)

40. She has a slight akquaintence with the arktic. (2)

41. Did you guys make all the arangements for the athaletes' party? (2)

42. The quire director can't stand even the slightest critacism. (2)

43. Last Chrissmus, we were confidunt the controvursy was over—boy, we're we wrong! (4)

44. By next Eester, we should no what the affect of the oil spill was on the envirunmunt. (4)

45. Mom's way to bizzy two go too the benifit. (5)

46. The principle wrote a safety pamplet, but no one read it. (2)

47. The lawyers proved in court that the goverment did'nt discrimenate against those wimen. (4)

48. Eveybody in our class got a free calender. (2)

49. For Haloween, I wore a gippsie costume. (2)

50. We herd the barbeque was canculled. (3)

51. Its aparent that there garuntee is'nt worth the paper its printed on. (6)

52. Do you think peeple were aktually effected buy that rumor? (4)

53. I'd just like a little acknowledgment of all hour hard work. (1)

54. When he found the cubberd was bare, the poor dog was definitly dissapointed. (3)

55. According to the police discription, that man is desperit! (2)

56. Thay found all the dimonds hidden in a box in the sematary. (3)

57. Evryone is elgible untill Febuary. (4)

58. She's the forth forinn athelete to try to stay on in the United States. (3)

59. In one more our, we'll finaly get home. (2)

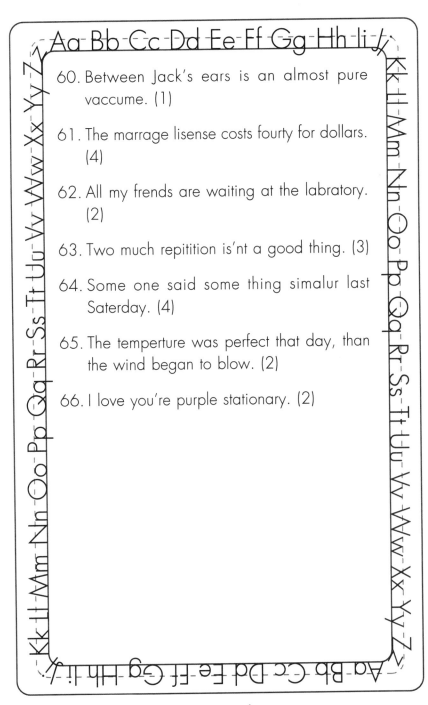

Aa Bb Cc Dd Ee Ff Gg Hh Ii Jj

60. Between Jack's ears is an almost pure vaccume. (1)

61. The marrage lisense costs fourty for dollars. (4)

62. All my frends are waiting at the labratory. (2)

63. Two much repitition is'nt a good thing. (3)

64. Some one said some thing simalur last Saterday. (4)

65. The temperture was perfect that day, than the wind began to blow. (2)

66. I love you're purple stationary. (2)

see pages 256–258 for answers

Chapter 18:
Exercise Answers

Chapter 3 Exercises

Exercise 1:

The errors are underlined: "English spelling is much too difficult. Consider words like these: see and sea, here and hear, to and too and two. Why should we put up with all these difficulties? What we need is a Revolution! Listen to our secret plan. First, we will use 's' instead of the soft 'c.' <u>Sertainly</u>, <u>sivil</u> servants in all <u>sities</u> will <u>resieve</u> this news with joy. The hard 'c' would then be <u>replased</u> by 'k' <u>sinse</u> both letters are <u>pronounsed</u> alike. This will not only <u>klear</u> up <u>konfusion</u> in the minds of <u>klerikal</u> workers, but typewriters and keyboards <u>kould</u> be made with one less letter. For our second step, we'll announce that the troublesome 'ph' will be written 'f.' This will make words like '<u>fotograf</u>' much shorter to write. In the third stage, <u>publik</u> <u>akseptanse</u> of the new spelling <u>kan</u> be <u>expekted</u> to reach the stage where more <u>komplikated</u> changes are possible. We will <u>enkourage</u> the removal of double letters which have always ben a <u>deterent</u> to <u>akurate</u> <u>speling</u>. We <u>al</u> <u>agre</u> that the <u>horible</u> <u>mes</u> of silent 'e's' in the <u>languag</u> is <u>disgrasful</u>. <u>Therefor</u>, we <u>kould</u> drop <u>thes</u> and <u>kontinu</u> to read and <u>writ</u> as though nothing had <u>hapend</u>. When <u>al</u> <u>thes</u> <u>changs</u> <u>ar</u> <u>akseptd</u>, people will be <u>reseptiv</u> to steps such as <u>replasing</u> 'th' by 'z.' Perhaps <u>zen</u> <u>ze</u> <u>funktion</u> of 'w' <u>kould</u> be taken on by 'v,' <u>vitsh</u> is, after <u>al</u>, half a 'w.' <u>Finaly</u>, <u>ze</u> <u>unesesary</u> 'o' <u>kuld</u> be <u>dropd</u> from <u>vords</u> <u>kontaining</u> 'ou'. Similar arguments <u>vud</u> of <u>kors</u> be <u>aplid</u> to <u>ozer</u> <u>kombinations</u> of <u>leters</u>. <u>Ve</u> <u>vud</u> <u>eventuli</u> <u>hav</u> a <u>reli</u> <u>sensibl</u> <u>riten</u> <u>stil</u>! <u>Zer</u> <u>vud</u> be no more <u>trubls</u> with <u>speling</u> and <u>evrion</u> <u>vud</u> <u>fin</u> it <u>ezi</u> <u>tu</u> <u>understan</u> <u>esh</u> <u>ozer</u>!"

Exercise 2: Soft Cs
certainly

civil

cities

receive

replaced

since

pronounced

acceptance

Double Letters, "Twins"
been

deterrent

accurate

spelling

all

agree

horrible

mess

happened

Cs that Sound Like Ks
clear

confusion

clerical

public

can

complicated

expected

encourage

could

containing

combinations

Silent *Es*

language

disgraceful

therefore

these

continue

write

changes

are

receptive

Chapter 6 Exercises

Exercise 1: They, There, Their, and They're

1. their

2. there

3. there

4. their

5. they're

6. there

7. their

8. there

9. they're

10. there

Exercise 2: Tricky Contractions

1. that's

2. it's

3. don't

4. doesn't

5. you're

6. let's

7. there's

Mistakes

1. its

2. it's

3. your

4. you're

5. theirs

6. there's

7. theirs

Chapter 7 Exercises

1. Easter

2. Everybody

3. Someone

4. always

5. Maybe, maybe

6. Christmas

7. Halloween

8. Saturday

9. everyone

10. something

11. Everything

12. sometime

13. Everywhere

14. anything

Chapter 8 Exercises

1. witch

2. went

3. which

4. too

5. two

6. to, buy

7. hour

8. our

9. through

10. except

11. no, no, no

12. probably, two

13. finally

14. Which

15. know, where, two

16. went, to, went through

17. accept

18. probably, finally, two

19. buy, except

20. which, where

Chapter 9 Exercises

1. Get, off

2. off

3. Until, really

4. really

5. than

6. favorite, especially

7. usually, different

8. heard, favorite

9. Different, different

10. again

11. especially

12. friends, again

13. friends, usually, around

14. favorite

15. heard, again

Review Test—The List of Fiendishly Hard Words

1. There, a lot

2. two

3. To, to, their

4. its

5. It's

6. Because, don't

7. They're, probably, Easter

8. They, you're

9. our, Christmas

10. Finally, off

11. Where, Halloween

12. didn't, until

13. buy

14. Let's, really

15. then

16. Usually, we're

17. Sometimes, went

18. through

19. Which, doesn't

20. heard, favorite

21. believe, again

22. accept, except

23. Everything, different

24. were, always, especially, Saturday

25. always, friends, everywhere

26. Maybe, everybody, you're

27. didn't, know

28. Someone, restaurant

29. There's, their, restaurant

Chapter 10 Exercises

1. affect

2. effect, effect, four

3. February, forth

4. Fourth

5. principal, forty

6. principal

7. lose

8. principal

9. loose

10. principle

11. loss, four

12. February

13. laboratory, fourth

14. four

15. February, principal, affected, loss

16. effect

17. forty, four, fourth

18. principles

19. loose

20. lose

Chapter 11 Exercises

1. fiery

2. busy, choir

3. gauge's

4. leopard, Sergeant

5. people

6. women

7. sophomore

8. woman

9. diamond

10. succeed, diamond

11. vacuum

12. leopard, woman

13. vacuum

14. women, fiery

15. people, choir

16. leopard, busy

17. gauge, people

18. sergeant, diamond

19. succeed, vacuum, gauge

20. woman, leopard, fiery, women

Chapter 12 Exercises

1. Actually, attempts

2. government, cupboard

3. environment

4. raspberry, plaid

5. Actually, recognize

6. Several, cupboard, surprised

7. yacht, temperature

8. government, environment

9. temperature, surprised

10. recognize, raspberry

11. surprised, yacht's, plaid

12. several, attempts, surprised

13. surprise, actually

14. several, attempts, temperature

15. government, yacht

16. raspberry, cupboard

17. environment, surprise

18. recognize, attempting

Chapter 13 Exercises

1. athlete

2. guarantee, license

3. judgment, immediately

4. convenient

5. nickel

6. occurred, guarantee

7. judgment, paid

8. athlete

9. foreign, guarantee

10. license, necessary

11. conveniently

12. nickels

13. immediately

14. occur

15. paid, omitted

Review Test for Chapters 10–13

1. February, principal, leopard

2. choir, diamond

3. woman sergeant

4. fiery, temperature

5. gauge, vacuum

6. For, fourth, people

7. guarantee, yachts

8. succeed, athlete, attempts

9. plaid, raspberry

10. laboratory, recognize

11. women, sophomores

12. Several foreign, cupboard

13. judgment, forty, diamonds

14. Several, athletes omitted

15. effect, environment

16. paid, for, guaranteed

17. people, immediately

18. convenient, principle

19. license, actually

20. occurred, surprised

Chapter 14 Exercises

1. marriage

2. pamphlets, nuclear

3. persistent, receive

4. too, personal

5. skillful, repetition

6. stationary, similar, stationary

7. whether, weather

8. personnel, received

9. nuclear

10. personal, marriage

11. weather, stationary

12. persistently, receives

13. pamphlet

14. whether, skillful

15. marriages, similar

Chapter 15 Answers

1. analysis, arrangement, benefited
2. appearance, disappointing
3. criticism
4. disappointed
5. controversy, eligible
6. confident, arrangement
7. apparent, desperate
8. criticism
9. disappointed
10. eligible
11. controversy
12. analysis
13. Apparently, appearance
14. desperate
15. benefited, disappointed

Chapter 16 Answers

1. barbecue, arctic
2. acquaintance, friend
3. to bury
4. discriminate
5. exceed
6. description
7. extension
8. fulfill
9. occasion
10. procedure
11. arctic, definitely
12. barbecue, bury
13. description, definitely
14. acquaintance
15. school, discrimination
16. extension
17. definitely, exceeded
18. occasion, fulfilled
19. procedure, cancels

The Official Spelling Smart Junior's Really, Really Tough Spelling Test for the Entire Book

1. occurred, immediately, off

2. paid, occasion

3. nickel, anything, they

4. judgment, personnel

5. recognize, rhythm

6. through, until, attempt

7. it's, convenient, everything

8. difference, loss

9. were, omitted

10. receive, something

11. You're, really, lose, too personally

12. know, where, went

13. height, twenty-four

14. woman, no, principles

15. They, procedure, probably

16. Because, their, appearance

17. always, fulfill

18. exceed, except

19. Which, women, there

20. assistant, bury

21. favorite, Raspberry, Surprise

22. Maybe, your, leopard

23. Let's, nuclear

24. succeed, necessary, persistent

25. different, extension

26. Doesn't, friendship, a lot, everywhere

27. Whether, there's, we're

28. don't, believe, immediately, let's, until, Saturday

29. Your, its, that's

30. Several, skillful

31. Sometimes, sophomore

32. stomachache, again

33. usually, around, a lot

34. weather, we're, yacht

35. woman, witch

36. We're, restaurant, Saturday

37. sergeant, especially, cancels, everybody's

38. gauge, for, buy

39. don't, accept, your, analysis, it's

40. acquaintance, arctic

41. arrangements, athletes'

42. choir, criticism

43. Christmas, confident, controversy, were

44. Easter, know, effect, environment

45. too, busy, to, to, benefit

46. principal, pamphlet

47. government, didn't, discriminate, women

48. Everybody, calendar

49. Halloween, gypsy

50. heard, barbecue, cancelled

51. It's, apparent, their, guarantee, isn't, it's

52. people, actually, affected, by

53. our

54. cupboard, definitely, disappointed

55. description, desperate

56. They, diamonds, cemetery

57. Everyone, eligible, until, February

58. fourth, foreign, athlete

59. hour, finally

60. vacuum

61. marriage, license, forty-four

62. friends, laboratory

63. Too, repetition, isn't

64. Someone, something, similar, Saturday

65. temperature, then

66. your, stationery

About the Author

Gary Arms, Ph.D., is an associate professor in the English Department of one of the Midwest's finest small colleges, Clarke College, in Dubuque, Iowa. He is the author of several plays as well as another book in this series, *Mythology Smart Junior*. Gary lives in a comfortable old house with his beautiful wife, Susie, and their sons Joe and David, the Wonder Boys.

notes

notes

notes

notes

notes

notes

notes

notes

notes

notes

notes

notes

FIND US...

International

Hong Kong
4/F Sun Hung Kai Centre
30 Harbour Road, Wan Chai,
Hong Kong
Tel: (011)85-2-517-3016

Japan
Fuji Building 40, 15-14
Sakuragaokacho, Shibuya Ku,
Tokyo 150, Japan
Tel: (011)81-3-3463-1343

Korea
Tae Young Bldg, 944-24,
Daechi- Dong, Kangnam-Ku
The Princeton Review- ANC
Seoul, Korea 135-280,
South Korea
Tel: (011)82-2-554-7763

Mexico City
PR Mex S De RL De Cv
Guanajuato 228 Col. Roma
06700 Mexico D.F., Mexico
Tel: 525-564-9468

Montreal
666 Sherbrooke St.
West, Suite 202
Montreal, QC H3A 1E7 Canada
Tel: (514) 499-0870

Pakistan
1 Bawa Park - 90 Upper Mall
Lahore, Pakistan
Tel: (011)92-42-571-2315

Spain
Pza. Castilla, 3 - 5° A, 28046
Madrid, Spain
Tel: (011)341-323-4212

Taiwan
155 Chung Hsiao East Road
Section 4 - 4th Floor,
Taipei R.O.C., Taiwan
Tel: (011)886-2-751-1243

Thailand
Building One, 99 Wireless Road
Bangkok, Thailand 10330
Tel: (662) 256-7080

Toronto
1240 Bay Street, Suite 300
Toronto M5R 2A7 Canada
Tel: (800) 495-7737
Tel: (716) 839-4391

Vancouver
4212 University Way NE,
Suite 204
Seattle, WA 98105
Tel: (206) 548-1100

National (U.S.)

We have over 60 offices around the U.S. and run courses in over 400 sites. For courses and locations within the U.S. call 1 (800) 2/Review and you will be routed to the nearest office.

Award-Winning
Smart Junior Guides
for Kids Grades 6-8
from THE PRINCETON REVIEW

AMERICAN HISTORY SMART JR.
0-679-77357-6
$10.00 paperback

ARCHAEOLOGY SMART JR.
0-679-77537-4
$10.00 paperback

ASTRONOMY SMART JR.
0-679-76906-4
$12.00 paperback

GEOGRAPHY SMART JR.
0-679-77522-6
$12.00 paperback

GRAMMAR SMART JR.
0-679-76212-4
$12.00 paperback

MATH SMART JR.
0-679-75935-2
$12.00 paperback

MATH SMART JR. II
0-679-78377-6
$10.00 paperback

MYTHOLOGY SMART JR.
0-679-78375-X
$10.00 paperback

READING SMART JR.
0-679-78376-8
$10.00 paperback

SPELLING SMART JR.
0-679-77538-2
$10.00 paperback

STUDY SMART JR.
0-679-77539-0
$10.00 paperback

WORD SMART JR.
0-679-75936-0
$12.00 paperback

WORD SMART JR. II
0-375-75030-4
$12.00 paperback

WRITING SMART JR.
0-679-76131-4
$12.00 paperback

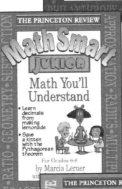

THE PRINCETON REVIEW
Word Smart Junior
Build a Straight "A" Vocabulary
- Feel dejected because you lack eloquence?
- Are sedulous reading assignments the bane of your existence?
Over 650 words that will transform you into a vocabulary virtuoso.
For Grades 6-8
by C. L. Brantley

THE PRINCETON REVIEW
Math Smart Junior
Math You'll Understand
- Learn decimals from making lemonade
- Save a kitten with the Pythagorean theorem
For Grades 6-8
by Marcia Lerner

THE PRINCETON REVIEW
Writing Smart Junior
The Art and Craft of Writing
- Never write another bad book report!
- Write stories and poems that will someday make you millions of dollars (maybe)!
For Grades 6-8
by C. L. Brantley

Bestselling
Smart Guides
for Students and Adults
from THE PRINCETON REVIEW

Biology Smart
0-679-76908-0
$12.00 paperback

Grammar Smart
0-679-74617-X
$11.00 paperback

Job Smart
0-679-77355-X
$12.00 paperback

Math Smart
0-679-74616-1
$12.00 paperback

Math Smart II
0-679-78383-0
$12.00 paperback

Math Smart for Business
0-679-77356-8
$12.00 paperback

Negotiate Smart
0-679-77871-3
$12.00 paperback

Reading Smart
0-679-75361-3
$12.00 paperback

Research Paper Smart
0-679-78382-2
$10.00 paperback

Speak Smart
0-679-77868-3
$10.00 paperback

Study Smart
0-679-73864-9
$12.00 paperback

Word Smart
0-679-74589-0
$12.00 paperback

Word Smart II
0-679-73863-0
$12.00 paperback

Word Smart for Business
0-679-78391-1
$12.00 paperback

Word Smart: Genius Edition
0-679-76457-7
$12.00 paperback

Work Smart
0-679-78388-1
$12.00 paperback

Writing Smart
0-679-75360-5
$12.00 paperback

Expert Advice

Talk About It

Pop Surveys

Paying for it

THE
PRINCETON
REVIEW

Getting in

Word du Jour

Find-O-Rama School & Career Search

www.review.com

Finding it

Best Schools